Research and Scholarly Integrity in Graduate Education:
A Comprehensive Approach

Research and Scholarly Integrity in Graduate Education: A Comprehensive Approach

This publication was prepared for the Council of Graduate Schools by Daniel Denecke, Julia Kent, and Jeff Allum. The publication and the project it describes were funded by a contract from the U.S. Department of Health and Human Services (#HHSP23320072208TC) and the Office of Research Integrity.

ISBN-10 1-933042-36-2
ISBN-13 978-1-933042-36-7

TABLE OF CONTENTS

CONTENTS

ACKNOWLEDGMENTS

The Project for Scholarly Integrity brought together individuals with unique backgrounds and perspectives from around the country. Senior administrators, faculty, researchers, students, and staff from across the research and scholarly communities of participating campuses all helped to define and develop the PSI, and to reflect upon individual programs as they evolved.

The authors would first like to thank the members of the PSI Advisory Board for providing substantive guidance at the beginning of this project: Edward Gabriel, Jeffery Gibeling, Clark Hulse, Greg Koski, Bryan D. Noe, Suzanne T. Ortega, Lawrence Rhoades, Adil Shamoo, Lisa A. Tedesco, and Robert E. Thach.

The graduate deans who served as principal investigators and their colleagues who served as project directors or co-PI's acted in multiple capacities as dedicated champions for a comprehensive approach to graduate education in research integrity and the responsible conduct of research. These individuals met regularly throughout the project together and with members of their campus teams, provided vision and leadership in project implementation and assessment, and shared the results of their projects in an ongoing way with the broader U.S. graduate community. We cannot express enough gratitude for their tireless efforts on their own campuses, their willingness to collaborate with each other, and their institutional and national leadership on this issue. These PSI leaders include: Suzanne Adair, Jan Allen, Carlos J. Alonso, Elizabeth Boyd, Andrew Comrie, Jeffrey Engler, Henry Foley, Melissa Gilstrap, Karen Klomparens, Michelle Lampl, Bryan D. Noe, Eva Pell, Henry Pinkham, Mark Risjord, Tina Tarin, Lisa A. Tedesco, and Regina Vasilatos-Younken.

This project would not have been possible without the strong support and leadership from key individuals at the Office of Research Integrity (ORI) and the Department of Health and Human Services (DHHS). We would especially like to thank our program officer Loc Nguyen-Khoa for his continued support, participation, and advice throughout the project, as well as John Dahlberg, John Galland, Larry Rhoades, Nick Steneck, Sandra Titus, and David Wright at ORI and Don Wright at DHHS.

We are very grateful to Carol Thrush, Brian Martinson, and the team that allowed us to test the feasibility of their climate survey for institutional review and improvement of graduate education in research and scholarly integrity. We are especially grateful to Carol and Brian for their willingness to devote time and effort over the course of the project to assisting CGS and individual institutions in addressing issues of implementation and analysis. Kurt Johnson and Brian Sonak of the survey research center provided assistance to institutions in survey administration and to CGS in aggregating institutional data. We thank Mark Frankel and the American Association for the Advancement of Science for their encouragement and for contributions to the PSI online resource base.

Others who have provided substantive input or assistance include: Melissa Anderson, Elizabeth Heitman, Sheila Kirby, and Scott Naftel.

Finally, we would like to thank our colleagues at CGS who provided invaluable input over the duration of the project: Robert Sowell, Debra W. Stewart, Diana Carlin, Joshua Mahler, Maureen Terese McCarthy, and Nancy Vincent.

FOREWORD

G raduate students in all research fields need explicit preparation in the standards of responsible research conduct (RCR), the skills of ethical reasoning, and the practice of scholarly integrity. For nearly a decade, the Council of Graduate Schools (CGS) has worked with U.S. universities to enhance the preparation of graduate students for the ethical challenges and responsibilities of scholarship and research. Since 2003, we have granted sub-awards to 22 universities (and worked with an additional 44 affiliate universities and colleges) to create graduate RCR education programs and resources. These projects have contributed to the development of early career researchers on each participating campus and to a broader national trend of providing high quality research integrity education during the formative stages of graduate students' professional development.

Two best practice guides document the results of our prior projects in this area. *Graduate Education for the Responsible Conduct of Research* (2006) reports on the results of a two-year project (2004-06) funded by the Office of Research Integrity (ORI) to develop and test interventions and assessment strategies at 10 institutions for the training of graduate students from the behavioral and biomedical sciences in the responsible conduct of research. A second publication, *Best Practices in Graduate Education for the Responsible Conduct of Research* (2009), describes results of a separate two-year project (2006-08) funded by a grant from the National Science Foundation (NSF) to develop cross-disciplinary programs in research ethics for students in science and engineering at eight institutions.

The current book is therefore the third CGS publication on the topics of building high quality RCR programs for graduate students and the leadership role of graduate schools in making these programs a success. It describes the Project for Scholarly Integrity, our most ambitious initiative in this area. With funding from ORI, CGS worked first with a planning committee and subsequently with six U.S. universities to define and develop a comprehensive approach to research and scholarly integrity.

During the timespan of this latest project, the national context for RCR education changed. In the early stages, advisory committee members believed strongly that the project should not be perceived as merely focused on "compliance": that is, it should not only be about helping individual students understand regulations or assisting universities to comply with RCR training requirements then in effect. What was needed were programs that also addressed a much broader set of issues: how to create and sustain an environment of trust and transparency between students and their advisors in the lab and elsewhere, how to ensure that students know where to go when they have questions, and how to make sure that institutions are efficiently providing the most effective and most relevant RCR training possible.

While the Project for Scholarly Integrity was underway, two major federal funders of U.S. research (the National Institutes of Health and the National Science Foundation) issued new requirements for graduate training in research integrity. Many institutions scrambled to put programs in place to comply with these more rigorous requirements. The universities in the PSI and prior CGS-sponsored projects were seen by many as "go to" sources of wisdom and expertise. They had already begun to develop programs that went beyond minimal requirements to address, more comprehensively, a wide range of graduate students' unmet needs.

The leadership of graduate deans and graduate schools has been essential to the development of the six model programs described in this book. Compliance with federal training requirements is essential, and graduate schools can help ensure that institutions meet the new NIH and NSF requirements. The goal embraced by these graduate schools was to ensure that our students have the knowledge and skills they need to conduct the highest quality research and advising needed to secure the continued public trust in American scholarship and to prepare future generations of scholars.

My hope is that the strategies and practices described in this publication prove helpful to those seeking practical models for RCR programs, innovative ideas for engaging the campus community in dialogue about key issues, and useful tools for ensuring that their efforts are responsive to the needs of students and faculty. I also hope this publication serves as a resource and a catalyst for enriched campus discussions of the needs and professional development of graduate students as well as of faculty and staff. CGS looks forward to continuing to assist all institutions as they seek to strengthen the role of the graduate school in fostering best practices in research and scholarly integrity.

Debra W. Stewart
President
Council of Graduate Schools

Introduction

Structured programs to train graduate students in research ethics and RCR are not new. Until recently, most universities have sought to provide as much of the required training as possible with online solutions. Although online training has practical advantages as one component of a good program, many also recognize the value and need for education programs that include face-to-face instruction and coverage of field-relevant topics. There are strong examples of U.S. programs that go beyond providing the bare minimum in RCR preparation.[1] These programs may offer workshops or seminar series, face-to-face research ethics training, brown bag discussions, or special courses or mini-courses. At many universities, some portion of graduate students already receive a hybrid of online and face-to-face training on topics such as human subjects protocols for obtaining informed consent, animal care and use, and research misconduct. In general, though, even where good programs exist, RCR education for graduate students has been limited in scope, often consisting of piecemeal or ad-hoc activities, and provided without a clear assessment plan.

The Project for Scholarly Integrity (PSI) is a CGS initiative to generate models for integrating research ethics and the responsible conduct of research (RCR) into graduate education. The PSI was funded by a contract from the Office of Research Integrity (ORI) within the context of its longer-term goal to infuse or embed RCR into the fabric of U.S. graduate education. Only when RCR education is embedded into institutional practices and graduate programs, and not merely seen as a perfunctory add-on or mere compliance requirement, will we begin to make real progress on the broader issues that lead to misbehavior and misconduct in research.

This publication describes the Project for Scholarly Integrity and the activities of six participating universities. It is intended to be useful to other institutions seeking to develop a comprehensive scholarly integrity program that

---

1. A few RCR programs that have been recognized for high quality offerings and national leadership, but by no means an exhaustive list, include: Duke University (http://gradschool.duke.edu/academics/degree_reqs/rcr/index.php), Georgia Tech (http://www.rcr.gatech.edu/), the University of San Diego (http://ethics.ucsd.edu/research.html), and the University of Michigan (http://research.umich.edu/policies/compliance-resources/).

prepares graduate students from different disciplines to be scholars and researchers who are well-informed about the professional expectations for responsible conduct of research and the ethical issues unique to their chosen field of study.

Graduate School Leadership in Shaping Quality Programs

Effective program leadership can be provided by individuals in a variety of different roles. RCR Directors, compliance office staff, faculty with expertise in research ethics, and graduate school staff with expertise in professional development of graduate students all play an important role in effective RCR programming. Even under strong leadership, however, programs that have gone beyond the minimal approach face common challenges. These challenges include:

- Overreliance on experts and underutilization of faculty in the disciplines to define program content and structure, or vice versa (underutilization of experts and overreliance on faculty without expertise on key topics);
- Overemphasis on one perspective (such as compliance training or ethical theory) at the expense of others, often as a result of charging one or a few individual(s) with directing campus efforts; and
- Lack of coordination between campus units that have different strengths and resources to offer, but which may be duplicating each other's efforts or not reaching their intended audiences.

Research ethics and RCR education programs also face challenges common to all graduate professional development programs, such as:

- How to scale up good practices to accommodate sufficient numbers of students,
- How to deliver content to meet the needs of students from different disciplines,
- How to gain faculty support for graduate student involvement, especially when faculty members may believe that they already provide sufficient coverage of RCR issues in their advising or in the lab setting, and
- How to coordinate and leverage effective existing activities to greatest effect.

The PSI project builds upon a decade of work with U.S. institutions that has sought to identify strategies for overcoming all of these challenges through graduate school engagement and leadership. In the absence of senior university leadership from the graduate school or other unit responsible for the overall quality of graduate education, even excellent programs can sometimes reach only handfuls of students in select fields. When led and coordinated by the graduate school, these programs have the potential to reach many more students. Indeed, some graduate schools have been instrumental in making education in research and scholarly integrity a requirement of all graduate students.[2]

Another advantage that graduate school leadership can provide is to ensure a breadth of programs to address student needs from a range of different disciplines. When the graduate school plays a lead role in structuring and sustaining these programs, and when it communicates the value of graduate education in responsible conduct of research and research integrity, the activities and resources developed have the potential to reach students from all relevant fields. Graduate schools can help ensure, for example, that central RCR resources on issues that cross disciplines, such as mentoring relationships and responsibilities, fairness in peer review, intellectual conflicts of interest, and intellectual property rights, are available to all students, while incentivizing better coverage of field-specific issues in colleges and/or programs.

Graduate school leadership of RCR programs can also help to address the challenge of building essential faculty support and participation. All of the PSI projects recognized the key role that faculty must play in providing input at various stages. Some experimented successfully with mini-grant programs to inspire curricular innovation and integration, while others successfully used assessment data and follow-up discussions with faculty to identify areas where graduate schools and programs could work together to meet student needs. Although faculty buy-in was consistently recognized as the main challenge to embedding research integrity into graduate education, it is the key to sustainable, meaningful progress.

Finally, graduate schools are in a unique position to assess and coordinate the activities of different campus units involved in graduate education in research ethics, RCR, and scholarly integrity, and to work with those units to enhance their complementarity. When people from across the institutions are working in tandem and communicating with each other, there is greater likelihood that the resulting programs will be embedded and sustained and that programmatic shortcomings are addressed.

---

2. Among universities that now require RCR training for all doctoral candidates are: Duke University, Emory University, and Pennsylvania State University.

Defining Characteristics of PSI Projects

The Project for Scholarly Integrity involved graduate school leadership in the planning, development, implementation, and assessment of comprehensive programs for graduate students in research and scholarly integrity. By "comprehensive," we do not mean that they cover every aspect of research ethics and research integrity or that they address every need or student within the institution. Rather, we use the term "comprehensive" to designate programs that have the following four characteristics in common:

- **They support a range of curricular approaches**, rather than being overly specialized (for example, focused on research compliance issues only or research ethics issues only);
- **They comprise an integrated and complementary suite of activities**, rather than a piecemeal assortment of mini-courses, lectures, and/or workshops;
- **They are far reaching**, involving a significant portion of students, faculty, and staff from across a wide array of fields and campus units and/or piloting interventions in the short term, with a plan for broader scale-up; and
- **They are informed by evidence**, both in the early stages through needs assessment and in the later stages through efforts to understand which interventions promise to be most and least effective.

This publication synthesizes the experience of six institutions and identifies key features of a comprehensive approach to graduate education in research and scholarly integrity. The goal of a program based on such an approach is, as one PSI university expressed it, "To move research integrity out from the shelter of the compliance office and into the general culture of the university." This does not mean minimizing the important role that the compliance office plays; to the contrary, it means bolstering that role through activities conducted in a coordinated way across the university. In the following pages, we describe a framework for institutional action and graduate school leadership that informed the proposals of U.S. institutions; we discuss promising practices and lessons learned from participants' experiences in key areas of program development such as project planning, implementation, and assessment; and we provide an overview of the assessment approach taken in the PSI, which was developed in collaboration with the six awardees and adopted across the project by all, with discussion of key findings that informed project improvements.

Building on Prior CGS Projects in the Responsible Conduct of Research

The Project for Scholarly Integrity is the third major CGS initiative to assist U.S. universities in developing, assessing, and enhancing programs in RCR, research integrity and research ethics. Like the prior RCR projects and other CGS best practice initiatives, the PSI involved sub-awards to universities whose funded activities consisted of both common activities and unique interventions, or innovations. In defining the common awardee requirements and activities, CGS drew from the literature on effective RCR education and lessons learned in two prior CGS RCR projects. In defining the unique interventions, graduate schools developed plans specific to their institutions' goals, organizational contexts, and environmental needs.

The first, ORI-funded CGS RCR initiative active 2004 to 2006 resulted in 10 projects to develop and evaluate RCR programs in graduate education (see Appendix A for a list of institutions and affiliates). The CGS publication *Graduate Education for the Responsible Conduct of Research* (2006) explores the rationale behind the development of graduate RCR programs and discusses six best practices for program start-up:

1. Establish an advisory board
2. Provide public forums
3. Offer two-tiered (discipline-based and university-wide) instruction
4. Teach ethical reasoning skills
5. Make RCR training mandatory
6. Develop multi-level assessment

The second CGS RCR initiative, funded by NSF, addressed the needs of students in science and engineering for greater understanding of professional standards in their disciplines and for enhanced skills in deliberate ethical reasoning about issues that arise in interdisciplinary research and in public-policy arenas. This grant program (active 2006 to 2008) resulted in six additional projects and expanded activities at two universities that had also participated in the initial ORI-funded initiative (listed in Appendix A). The resulting publication, *Best Practices in Graduate Education for the Responsible Conduct of Research* (2009), recommends that institutions:

1. Build on existing resources and programs
2. Use experts (such as "ethics center" faculty and staff or philosophy faculty) alone, or in partnership with core science faculty, to teach ethical deliberation

3. Use assessment results, including any disparities in results from different groups (such as graduate students and faculty) to generate awareness and support for reforms

4. Sequence requirements for RCR training to coincide with stages of student progress toward degree

5. Combine cost-effective online resources with the more effective face-to-face activities (i.e., don't limit student exposure to online resources only)

That 2009 publication also includes recommendations for optimizing programs at doctoral and master's-focused institutions.

In January 2008, CGS appointed a planning committee charged to assist in identifying the requisite components of a comprehensive institutional approach to embedding research integrity across graduate education. The planning committee was composed, with input from ORI, of graduate deans from six major research universities and national RCR experts recommended to CGS by ORI.[3] The committee met three times in 2008 to develop and review a framework document that distilled lessons from prior CGS projects and drew from current knowledge of promising practices in RCR program design and strategies for achieving culture change. The deans who served on the planning committee were selected from institutions that made a significant impact on the education and training of biomedical and behavioral researchers. They also included individuals who had strong personal track records for successfully implementing graduate education reforms at their respective universities.

The resulting PSI Framework Document accompanied the Request for Proposals (RFP) issued in April 2008 and was presented as a supplemental guide for proposal development. In addition to building in some of the

---

3. Dean and RCR experts included: Jeffery Gibeling, Dean of Graduate Studies, University of California, Davis; Clark Hulse, Associate Chancellor, Dean of the Graduate College, University of Illinois at Chicago; Bryan D. Noe, Dean, Graduate School, University of Alabama at Birmingham; Suzanne T. Ortega, Vice Provost and Dean, Graduate School, University of Washington; Adil Shamoo, Department of Biochemistry and Molecular Biology, University of Maryland, Baltimore; Lisa A. Tedesco, Vice Provost, Academic Affairs/Dean, Graduate School, Emory University; Robert E. Thach, Dean, Graduate School of Arts and Sciences, Washington University; Greg Koski, Senior Scientist, Institute for Health Policy, Massachusetts General Hospital and Associate Professor, Department of Anesthesiology and Critical Care, Harvard Medical School was recommended by ORI and served as an external subject expert on the committee. Program Officers Edward Gabriel and Lawrence Rhoades from ORI and CGS staff members Diana Carlin, Daniel Denecke, Robert Sowell, Debra Stewart, and Nancy Vincent also participated.

promising practices identified in prior projects as minimum commitments and requirements, the RFP encouraged further investigation into areas where more attention was needed: interdisciplinary activity, intercultural activity, and interaction between units and groups.

Institutional Partners in the PSI

An external review committee was selected to review proposals on the basis that (a) reviewers' institutions had not submitted proposals to participate in this project and (b) they met one or more of the following criteria: they had served on the planning committee for the project; they had served as a graduate dean on a successful university project funded from a prior CGS RCR project; they have nationally recognized expertise in RCR; and/or they had led, as graduate dean, an initiative at their university that strategically and successfully addressed an issue of importance in graduate education. Also participating with the review committee, as non-voting members, were the program officer from ORI and CGS project staff. CGS project staff developed a Proposal Review Rubric used by committee members to select the institutions that received sub-contracts.

The strengths and weaknesses of twenty submissions were evaluated, of which six were selected to develop model PSI programs. PSI institutions included:

- Columbia University
- Emory University
- Michigan State University (MSU) (*)
- Pennsylvania State University (PSU) (*)
- The University of Alabama at Birmingham (UAB), and
- The University of Arizona

Those universities that submitted proposals, but which were not among the six awardees, were invited to participate as PSI affiliates (listed in Appendix A). Many of these affiliates proceeded with at least a portion of their

---

* MSU and PSU collaborated with a third institution, the University of Wisconsin-Madison, on a three-university consortium project. The University of Wisconsin elected not to receive funding for their participation and hence did not submit reports or assessment data. While this publication does not include results from the University of Wisconsin's project activities, that institution's efforts nevertheless informed the project in important ways and particularly enhanced the assessment efforts of funded partners described in detail in Part III.

plans using internal funding. Additionally, affiliates participated in open PSI discussions, the CGS PSI annual meeting and summer workshop sessions, and institutional assessment activities.

Although the PSI benefited, and encouraged participation of both affiliate and awardee universities, the results here primarily reflect the activities and data of the six awardee institutions.

Terms and Definitions

While terms such as "research ethics," "research integrity," and "responsible conduct of research" are sometimes used interchangeably, in this publication they are used to designate particular approaches and curricular content. The term "scholarly integrity" is intended to encompass all of these approaches. The following definitions are not meant to be prescriptive or absolute. Indeed, just as the use of these terms varies in different countries, terminology varied across the participating institutions. Rather, the definitions below are provided as a general guide to readers on how these key terms will be used in the following chapters.

Responsible Conduct of Research

The term "Responsible Conduct of Research" was adopted in 1989 by the Institute of Medicine in a report on reforms needed in U.S. health sciences education (IOM, 1989). Since then, it has been widely used to designate the specific areas in which researchers are expected to follow the professional codes and disciplinary norms, government regulations, and institutional policies for responsible research conduct (Steneck, 2007). ORI has used this term (and its abbreviation RCR) to refer to standards and expectations for conduct in Public Health Service (PHS) funded research. The textbook *An Introduction to the Responsible Conduct of Research* (2004, revised 2007) identifies nine "core areas" of RCR:

- Data Acquisition, Management, Sharing and Ownership
- Conflict of Interest and Commitment
- Human Subjects
- Animal Care
- Research Misconduct (*see definition below*)
- Publication Practices and Responsible Authorship
- Mentor/Trainee Responsibilities

- Peer Review
- Collaborative Science

Justifiably or not, perhaps because of the term's origins, "RCR" has sometimes been interpreted to mean narrow "training" in compliance with the rules of regulatory bodies. It has also sometimes been perceived as pertinent solely to NIH-funded fields. In recent years, however, RCR has been used more broadly to refer to education in research integrity for students and researchers including and beyond the biological and behavioral sciences. RCR has also expanded beyond the nine areas listed above to include topics such as: laboratory management, fiscal responsibility, hazardous materials, intellectual property (inventions, patents, and technology transfer), harassment prevention and complaint procedure, and the social impact of research.[4] Many of the educational activities in the PSI include curricular content that may be described as RCR.

Research Misconduct

A core subtopic of RCR is research misconduct. ORI defines "research misconduct" as "fabrication, falsification, or plagiarism in proposing, performing, or reviewing research, or in reporting research results," and elaborates:

"(a) Fabrication is making up data or results and recording or reporting them.
(b) Falsification is manipulating research materials, equipment, or processes, or changing or omitting data or results such that the research is not accurately represented in the research record.
(c) Plagiarism is the appropriation of another person's ideas, processes, results, or words without giving appropriate credit.
(d) Research misconduct does not include honest error or differences of opinion." (ORI, 2011)

While this federal definition of research misconduct has been considered for revision several times in recent decades, the core elements of falsification, fabrication and plagiarism (FFP) and intent to deceive have remained the essence of the federal definition of research misconduct.

---

4. See, for example, the memorandum from Bell and James (2011) regarding updates to RCR training (http://gradschool.duke.edu/documents/academics/2011-3-01%20Duke%20 RCR%20NIH-NSF%20summ.pdf).

Research Integrity

Research integrity is a term typically used to apply to a broader range of topics than individual misconduct. The 2002 National Academies report, *Integrity in Scientific Research*, for example, defines research integrity in terms of characteristics of both individual researchers and their institutions: "For the individual scientist, integrity embodies above all a commitment to intellectual honesty and personal responsibility for one's actions and to a range of practices that characterize responsible research conduct. These practices include:

- intellectual honesty in proposing, performing, and reporting research;
- accuracy in representing contributions to research proposals and reports;
- fairness in peer review;
- collegiality in scientific interactions, including communications and sharing of resources;
- transparency in conflicts of interest or potential conflicts of interest;
- protection of human subjects in the conduct of research;
- humane care of animals in the conduct of research; and
- adherence to the mutual responsibilities between investigators and their research teams" (National Research Council of the National Academies, 2002, p. 5)

Institutions "seeking to create an environment that promotes responsible conduct by individual scientists and that fosters integrity must establish and continuously monitor structures, processes, policies, and procedures that:

- provide leadership in support of responsible conduct of research;
- encourage respect for everyone involved in the research enterprise;
- promote productive interactions between trainees and mentors;
- advocate adherence to the rules regarding all aspects of the conduct of research, especially research involving human subjects and animals;
- anticipate, reveal, and manage individual and institutional conflicts of interest;
- arrange timely and thorough inquiries and investigations of allegations of scientific misconduct and apply appropriate administrative sanctions;
- offer educational opportunities pertaining to integrity in the conduct of research; and
- monitor and evaluate the institutional environment supporting integrity in the conduct of research and use this knowledge for continuous quality improvement." (ibid.)

Given the importance of institutional policies, leadership, assessment and climate to upholding the highest standards of research integrity in individual conduct, graduate deans play a critical role in creating and supporting the environments in which programs can succeed.

Research Ethics

The term research ethics is variously used to refer to the overarching area of study that encompasses RCR, to the ethical principles underlying the professional standards and rules for responsible conduct of research, and to the principles that can help researchers adjudicate and make decisions when values may be in conflict. In this book, the term is used in the latter sense. Whether students pursue academic or non-academic careers, understanding regulations, standards, and codes of conduct in their field of study is necessary, but insufficient. Both as students and as professionals in research careers, these individuals will also face situations that require them to make ethical decisions. Some of these situations will not present easy solutions but will rather call for ethical reasoning skills and the ability to weigh conflicting ethical claims with a sense of broader responsibility as citizens and scholars.

Scholarly Integrity

The planning committee for this project discussed at length issues of how universities might "brand" their efforts on campus for greatest impact, and the implications of using the different terms described above. The committee felt that the project name should reflect the broadest possible scope of institutional objectives and should resonate across different disciplines or fields. "Scholarly integrity" was suggested as an umbrella term for a variety of approaches that may differ in emphasis among research ethics, research integrity, and the responsible conduct of research. The term "scholarly integrity" was therefore adopted for this project and is intended to encompass *both* research integrity *and* the ethical understanding and skills required of researchers/scholars in domestic, international, and multicultural contexts. It is also intended to address ethical aspects of scholarship that influence the next generation of researchers as teachers, mentors, supervisors, and successful stewards of grant funds. At the same time, it was seen as a term that would also reinforce the core mission of research integrity that ORI as the sponsoring organization sought to advance by funding this project.

The Structure of this Book

This book is divided into three parts.

Part I discusses the broader context for PSI programs and activities. *Chapter 1* provides a background for the context in which graduate education for RCR programs exist. It summarizes recent changes in federal compliance requirements for universities and researchers, and it highlights factors in the broader research environment that have implications for optimizing RCR program development through a PSI approach. *Chapter 2* summarizes the results of the planning committee discussions about the essential ingredients of a comprehensive approach to integrating and institutionalizing RCR in graduate education. It discusses three "design principles" for a PSI approach to research integrity and research ethics. *Chapter 3* outlines a "Framework for Collaborative Action" encompassing five action areas that participants would be encouraged to plan, detail in their proposals, and follow in their projects. The chapters in Part II describe the actual activities of participating universities and roughly follow the outline of the action steps articulated in the PSI Framework Document.

Part II highlights promising practices and lessons learned from the six participating universities as they designed, implemented and assessed comprehensive programs in research and scholarly integrity. It also discusses midcourse adjustments made by the universities in response to the identification of new campus needs resulting from the assessment activities and close communication with other campus units. Readers looking for "nuts and bolts" strategies and ideas that can be implemented quickly may wish to begin with Part II.

A common assessment strategy was an essential component of this project, and distinguished it from prior CGS RCR initiatives. Part III outlines the assessment strategy used by participating universities, and discusses the instruments adopted. Here, we also discuss some of the key findings and their implications for the development and improvement of graduate education programs in research and scholarly integrity. The assessment results enabled graduate schools to provide greater focus, in campus discussions of RCR activities and resources, on specific campus needs. Use of common instruments across the project also facilitated the exchange of information about needs and resources and laid the groundwork for future benchmarking among campuses (and, on those campuses, among programs) in areas such as institutional climate for research integrity and curricular content. Assessments and evidence-based discussions that take into account perspectives and practices of faculty and students provide the essential foundation for the PSI approach. The results included here and on the companion online interactive data tool, the PSI Dashboard (http://www.cgsnet.org/benchmarking/best-practices-data/PSI-dashboard), are presented with guidelines for their use to help graduate schools shape and enhance programs to meet graduate student needs.

Together, Parts II and III, combined with the appendices, provide a menu of options and resources that campus leaders, faculty and staff can consider for adoption and adaptation. The publication discusses resources created by CGS or adopted by participants. These resources can be used to prompt and facilitate discussions between graduate schools and faculty regarding curricular needs assessment and curricular examples. The publication concludes with a discussion in Part IV of two online resources developed for the project, the PSI Dashboard and the PSI website (www.scholarlyintegrity.org), which together contain a wealth of tools, data, and resources for the development and enhancement of RCR programs.

The emphasis here is on recommended institutional processes and strategies for developing comprehensive research and scholarly integrity programs. The book describes the PSI approach to graduate education in research and scholarly integrity. It should be emphasized, however, that the PSI approach is not "one size fits all." Rather, the framework of design principles and action areas, and the lessons learned shared by PSI institutions, are intended to inspire others to structure campus discussions about what is both optimal and feasible at their institutions. We anticipate that as the community of institutions adopting a PSI approach expands, the lessons learned about the effectiveness of specific strategies taken by PSI institutions and the curricular content of these programs will evolve in ways that will continue to benefit institutions and graduate students.

PART I

Planning a Comprehensive Program for Graduate Education in Research and Scholarly Integrity

Chapter 1.
Why Graduate Education for Research and Scholarly Integrity?

While scholarly integrity programs are in principle relevant to and evolving to encompass all fields, traditionally they have focused on students in the sciences and engineering. To both the public and to individuals who embark on careers in education and research, science represents many of our highest aspirations.[5] Scientists seek to understand how things work; to discover and uphold the truth, even when it challenges conventional beliefs; to benefit society; and to solve the world's most pressing intellectual and practical problems. Science, and research across all disciplines, is also a highly social activity. The social structures that make scientific discovery possible are competitive, and the excitement of competition drives discovery. But these social structures are also collaborative and collective, requiring individual researchers often to work in teams and always to contribute to the larger communal enterprise of scholarship and research. The public benefits of science make headlines every day, and the public's conception of a scientist typically includes the personality traits of honesty, altruism, and objectivity to complement the highest levels of educational achievement. "Scientist" has therefore regularly ranked among the top professions in terms of public confidence and esteem.

This public esteem for scientists has carried over to the institutions and the leaders of those institutions. The National Science Board's *Science and Engineering Indicators* (2002) found "Public Confidence of Leadership in Se-

---

5. Chapters 1 through 3 include revised material from "The Project for Scholarly Integrity in Graduate Education: A Framework for Collaborative Action" (2008) prepared for the Council of Graduate Schools by Daniel D. Denecke that addresses the compelling need for a more comprehensive approach to scholarly integrity and identifies core issues that institutions need to address as they embark on such a project. The planning committee described in the introduction provided valuable input that informed and that paper.

lected Institutions" from 1973-2010 to be highest for the military, medicine and the scientific community, above that of the Supreme Court, education, and the press. In the 2010 indicators, the confidence expressed in the science profession and its institutions remained near its highest levels. Overall, what is often described as the compact or covenant between science and society has been a successful one. Through this compact, public funds support scientific endeavors that in turn benefit the public through applications and education. The foundation of this compact is integrity.

In the broader academic context, integrity is a concept that encompasses understanding the minimal standards of compliance in research, the personal ethical decision-making processes of individuals, and ultimately the ways in which our institutions reflect the highest aspirations and broadest commitment on the part of the academic profession to the principles of truth, scholarship, and the responsible education of future scholars. Whenever integrity by any of these definitions is compromised, the breach of trust that can result has important consequences for the individual researchers, the institutions they represent, and society. Research integrity is not simply an individual value, it is also an institutional value reflected in the culture that is reinforced by the processes in place and the daily decisions of individual researchers, faculty and mentors, campus leaders, and administrative staff.

A Changing Context for Research and Scholarship

Current efforts to improve the education of future scholars in the principles and practices of research integrity are important in the context of several phenomena: (a) an increase in the number of reported cases of misconduct, nationally and internationally; (b) the encroachment of external pressures upon academic research as interaction and interdependence intensifies among academic, commercial, and government sectors; and (c) the expanding scope of researchers' responsibilities as a consequence of the globalization of the scientific community. The growing interaction among academic, business, and government sectors and the globalization of the scientific community both have the potential to provide enormous public benefits, but they also will present the next generation of scholars with new challenges. University leaders and scholars now must work together to ensure that a strong tradition of research integrity evolves to meet these new challenges.

Compliance, Misconduct, and Misbehavior

Advocates of enhancing education in research integrity frequently argue that incidents of misconduct threaten to undermine the public confidence in science. Of course, the research community has had its share of highly visible incidents of research misconduct. Most of these cases fall under the categories of plagiarism and the falsification and fabrication of data.

Some of the most well-known cases in the U.S. over the last 25 years involve established researchers at prestigious universities and national labs. While these incidents have captured the public attention, the popular press has, for the most part, laid the responsibility for them on the moral lapses of a few individuals. When cases of research misconduct attract attention, however, institutional leaders and the university name are also subject to public scrutiny, for it is often the names of the institutions and not the individuals that appear in newspaper headlines.

One criticism where leadership is lacking is that even when universities have policies that establish clear consequences for misconduct and misbehavior, those policies are not always uniformly enforced. A concern about institutional reputation may account for some of the discrepancies between the articulation of university ethics policies and their implementation. Some administrators may fear that bringing cases of misconduct out into the open could jeopardize the reputation of their university. Despite the high visibility of the misconduct cases that have shaken the scientific community, the 2010 survey results noted above show that these do not appear to have had much of an effect on public confidence in science.[6] A recent rise in allegations and cases of misconduct suggests, however, that far beyond the mistakes and possible moral lapses of the few, there may also be systemic or cultural forces at work that, if left unanswered, could adversely affect the entire research enterprise.[7]

Yet serious misconduct cases can also present universities with opportunities to demonstrate the stakes behind research integrity education. Graduate deans and other senior administrators such as presidents, chancellors, provosts, and vice presidents for research and division deans can use these cases to highlight institutional vulnerabilities. They can also use these incidents as

---

6. A 2006 Harris Poll found that the integrity of scientists is highly regarded by the public. Scientists rank among the top three professions regarded as "most honest" (at 77%), behind only doctors (85%) and teachers (83%) (Harris Interactive, 2006), http://www.harrisinteractive.com/harris_poll/index.asp?PID=688.

opportunities to hold more overarching campus-wide conversations about the role of integrity in the mission of the university and the fundamental importance of academic integrity across all sectors of the university. Under true leadership, research misconduct can prompt heightened campus awareness about the need for improved education in research and scholarly integrity and of the causes and consequences of misconduct and misbehavior.

Impact of External Pressures on the New Research Culture

Systematic improvements are needed to uphold professional standards, but also to prepare individuals for the evolving complexity of the world of science and the place of the university in society (Casadevall and Fang, 2012). Transformations in both of these areas require a comparable evolution in our educational approach to preparing the next generation of scholars. A more systematic approach than has been undertaken in the past, under the guidance of senior leaders, is crucial now because of changing dynamics in the broader research culture in the last half-century.

The American university was once celebrated for being relatively sheltered from the external factors that can sometimes be perceived as providing incentives for misconduct. In *Science, The Endless Frontier*, his report to Harry S. Truman in July 1945 (requested a year earlier by President Franklin D. Roosevelt), Vannevar Bush asserted that America's colleges and universities "are uniquely qualified by tradition and by their special characteristics to carry on basic research." Within these institutions, "scientists may work in an atmosphere which is relatively free from the adverse pressure of convention, prejudice, or commercial necessity. At their best they provide the scientific worker with a strong sense of solidarity and security, as well as a substantial degree of personal intellectual freedom" (Bush, 1945).

But the overall context and climate for university research has changed, and the research enterprise is no longer as immune to the "adverse pressures" that Vannevar Bush identified a half-century ago. One of the key responsibilities of all educators is therefore to prepare students to thrive with integrity and professionalism in this more complex environment.

---

7. Office of Inspector General, National Science Foundation. Semiannual report to Congress, September 2011 (http://www.nsf.gov/pubs/2012/oig12001/oig12001.pdf). See also Fanelli (2009).

A number of external pressures on scientists, for example, are arguably strengthening incentives to "misbehave." Influential reports have encouraged stakeholders to work together to recognize "the role of the 'system' in contributing to incidences of research misconduct" (AAAS & ORI, 2000, p. 2).

Among the factors that influence the current system, or research culture, are[8]:

- Diminishing success rates for research grants leading to increased competition for funding;
- Diminishing national investments in education and training that do not keep up with increases in R&D investments.
- Commercial and political pressures that threaten the principles of disinterest and objectivity upon which scientific integrity is based.
- An ever-contracting "half-life" of knowledge, where the pace of discovery is accelerating at the same time that the average age of first tenure appointments and the average time spent in postdoctoral appointments is increasing.

The rapid pace of modern research compounded by the increased competition for grant funds creates additional pressure for conclusive findings, and the prompt publication of those findings diminishes the time and communal incentive for the self-regulatory processes of science to operate, via the replication and verification of experiments. New technologies that make research misbehavior more easily discernible also make it easier. There are different ways to respond to these changes, including policy reform and improvements in oversight. One response that is at least partly in the purview of graduate schools is to encourage greater awareness and frank discussions of these pressures among younger scholars, and to try to provide counterincentives where possible.

Globalization

Today, there are unprecedented opportunities for one's research to produce broad public benefits on a global scale. However, these opportunities also bring further pressures on researchers consequent with:

---

8. This list modifies and expands upon factors identified in the Lisbon report (Mayer and Steneck, 2007, p. 24).

- A research community that is quickly globalizing, but in which cultural differences are sometimes pronounced and not always fully understood by all parties;
- An increase in national R&D budgets globally that increases international competition in research; and
- Global teams that are increasingly called upon to address life or death issues concerning the environment, global public health, and security/anti-terrorism, among others, where errors and misconduct have potentially greater consequence and are more publicly visible than before.

Awareness of these trends is important, but it is not enough. Graduate students entering research careers in an increasingly global context arguably need to be prepared with new skills in areas that have typically not received sufficient emphasis in RCR programs. Increasingly, for example, research on a variety of topics with global applications requires scholars who can work effectively in interdisciplinary, inter-institutional, and international teams. Such research also requires researchers who are sensitive to the ethical issues surrounding the sometimes unintended global uses and different cultural contexts that the products of one's research may encounter.[9]

One challenge is the difficulty of integrating long-term and unintended consequences into RCR training and research ethics education, especially where such training has focused on compliance issues and students' understanding of standards and regulations. Here, supplementing a compliance approach with a values approach can be beneficial. Models of education in RCR, still largely focused on a traditional ethics that emphasizes short term ends in the immediate research setting may not yet be adequate to address the complexities of working in an intercultural and international context, where the consequences of one's research may lie outside one's immediate proximity, both geographically and temporally (Jonas, 1984). Ensuring the adequacy of our ethical models is especially important where life and death issues are concerned and where the consequences of responsible and irresponsible conduct are magnified. A comprehensive, values-based approach to research integrity will help the scholars we are now preparing in our graduate programs rise above these pressures and face ethical challenges with confidence.

---

9. In October, 2011, CGS launched a three-year project funded by a grant from NSF's EESE program to support the integration of research ethics education into graduate international collaborations. For more information, see: http://www.cgsnet.org/modeling-effective-research-ethics-education-graduate-international-collaborations

Summary

Important progress has already been made in improving the preparation of graduate students in RCR through projects supported by the Office of Research Integrity (ORI) and the National Science Foundation (NSF), including ORI- and NSF-sponsored projects of the Council of Graduate Schools.[10] The aims of the CGS Project for Scholarly Integrity also support the advancement of the responsible conduct of research, but have been broader and more inclusive than prior efforts. The project sought—and seeks— to leverage the U.S. graduate schools' unique capacity to lead in the review and revision of university policies, to assess and influence the institutional climate for research integrity, and use assessment data to foster collaborations between centralized units and faculty-led efforts in the disciplines or programs.

A long term goal of this project is to enhance research integrity by enhancing the preparation of graduate students. Increased compliance with professional standards by individual researchers would be difficult to measure within the time period of this project. An assumption underlying the project, however, is that as the educational approach developed here is adopted across U.S. institutions, a community of scholars will emerge that is on the whole more compliant. As the next chapter will show, the road to compliance is based in large part on a deeper understanding of the stakes surrounding research integrity, a personal and professional investment in maintaining high standards, and greater awareness of the complexity and intellectual challenges involved in resolving the ethical issues that arise in research.

---

10. See the web resources of ORI (http://ori.dhhs.gov/education/rcr_resources.shtml), NSF (http://www.nsf.gov/funding/pgm_summ.jsp?pims_id=13338), and CGS (www.cgsnet.org). See also, *Graduate Education for the Responsible Conduct of Research* (CGS, 2006) and Nicholas Steneck, *An Introduction to the Responsible Conduct of Research* (ORI 2007).

Chapter 2.
Principles of
Program Design

I n their study of national R&D labs, *Limited by Design*, Michael Crow and
Barry Bozeman conclude that success in research and development depends
as much upon the organizational characteristics and the collaboration of
scientists, administrators, and policymakers as on the research achievements
of individual lab scientists (1998). Similarly, the planning phase of the PSI
included the identification of "design principles" that would encourage
collaboration and contribute to effective research integrity programs. Three
"design principles" were established to guide the development of model
programs in embedding research and scholarly integrity into graduate
education. PSI programs were recommended to be:

1) Designed in such a way as to supplement, if not supplant, a compliance-based approach with a values-based approach to RCR education;
2) Informed by needs assessment and the activities evaluated and revisited in light of the evidence that arises from that assessment; and
3) As comprehensive as possible in terms of reaching students across
   disciplines, coordinating efforts of multiple units across campus, and
   meeting students' diverse needs for skills and understanding in RCR,
   research and scholarly integrity, and research ethics.

Building successful programs with these design principles in mind requires
leadership and coordination across campus units. It was therefore natural that
graduate schools would take the lead in their development.

A Values-based Approach

Among the recommendations that emerged from a recent global conference on research ethics was the need for nations and institutions to strike
a balance between "compliance-based" and a "values-based" approaches in
their policies and programs (CFRS, 2008). The call for more emphasis on the
latter is not intended to minimize the importance of compliance with U.S. federal rules and professional standards for responsible research conduct. Federal
agencies, like the leadership of U.S. graduate schools and universities, are justifiably concerned about the number of reported incidents of misconduct, per-
vasive patterns of misbehavior, and the financial and reputational costs related
to such misbehavior. The National Institutes of Health (NIH) and National
Science Foundation (NSF) recently required that recipients of federal funding
involving graduate students and/or postdocs include education and training
activities in responsible and ethical conduct of research.[11] The requirements in
the NIH update, and the materials issued by NSF supplemental to the recent
training mandate, send a clear signal that earlier institutional approaches to
providing minimal training will no longer suffice.

A values-based approach to graduate education in research integrity and
professionalism is necessary, however, both to obtain the essential support of
research faculty and to render compliance-based efforts more effective. Recently, researchers have emphasized the need to expand our definitions of ethical research behavior, and this expansion has important implications for the
role that institutions can play in providing a policy and educational environment that encourages responsible and ethical conduct of research.[12] A values-
based approach to addressing research integrity may require a serious assessment of the campus climate and difficult conversations about the factors within
the university and the broader research environment that may contribute to
misconduct as well as those that reinforce academic integrity.

While most of the public attention has fallen on sanctionable offenses in
falsification, fabrication, and plagiarism, and training has largely focused on
compliance in these areas, important discussions are taking place in the scien-

---

11. For information on the NIH update, see: http://grants.nih.gov/grants/guide/notice-files/
    not-od-10-019.html. For information on the NSF requirement, see: http://www.nsf.gov/
    pubs/policydocs/rcr/faqs_mar10.pdf.
12. See Martinson, Anderson, and de Vries (2005). See also Epstein, (2006), http://www.
    insidehighered.com/news/2006/04/24/science; AAAS & ORI, (2000); and Mayer and
    Steneck, (2007, p.7).

tific community about the prevalence of a wider range of questionable research practices including laboratory, data, financial, and classroom management. Addressing the full gamut of professional responsibilities of scholars requires a fundamental change in traditional ways of providing research ethics education.

An Evidence-based Approach

The PSI was distinct from prior CGS projects in RCR in that universities adopted a common assessment framework and, where possible, common instruments to assist graduate schools in their efforts to base program enhancements on evidence of success and need. The assessment approach was intended to provide graduate schools and those with whom they partnered on this project with a means of understanding where the gaps were, of evaluating the effectiveness of their programs over time, and of informing discussions with campus stakeholders.

Prior CGS projects encouraged participating universities to develop pilot instruments and approaches in these areas, and these tools influenced the approach taken by the PSI. *Best Practices in the Responsible Conduct of Research* (CGS, 2009), for example, discussed existing resources for assessing RCR and called for assessment to be developed in four areas: institutional practices, institutional climate, individual learning, and the prevalence of misconduct and misbehavior in research and/or of perceptions of such misbehavior and misconduct. The PSI was the first CGS initiative to develop and/or encourage the adoption of common instruments for assessment in two areas, respectively: the assessment of activities and resources and the assessment of institutional climate. A third area, learning, was designated as a target for future adoption of a common approach once a suitable instrument was agreed upon that could encompass all or part of the goals for content knowledge and/ or skills in research and scholarly integrity.

Chapter 8 discusses the importance of developing a communication strategy around assessment in scholarly integrity programs. Part III discusses the results of the project's baseline assessment of activities and resources and of institutional climate. (As noted in the introduction, an online benchmarking tool allows users to run custom analyses of PSI aggregated baseline data. This tool is intended to assist institutions considering adoption of PSI assessment instruments or similar tools to assess campus needs. Available at: www.cgsnet. org/benchmarking/best-practices-data/PSI-dashboard)

A Comprehensive Approach

The CGS Project for Scholarly Integrity in Graduate Education focused on the leadership of graduate schools and graduate deans in fostering responsible and quality scholarship through systematic improvements in graduate education. The primary emphasis of this project is on enhancing the education of individual graduate students in research integrity. This project also developed in response to the need to address "institutional and systematic structures" and the ways in which these structures shape behavioral patterns and individual decision-making processes. Because of the influence of institutional factors such as the policy environment and institutional climate on individual behavior, comprehensive reform would address the responsibilities not only of individual researchers but also of institutions and institutional leaders who have the capacity to influence those institutional factors.

The activities undertaken by CGS and PSI participating universities spanned every discipline. Because ORI provided funding for the project, the core target beneficiaries were graduate students in the biomedical and behavioral sciences. However, as the project evolved, every awardee university elected to scale up many of their proposed activities to reach across the disciplines, both because this was resonant with the existing priorities of the institutions, all of whom contributed resources well in excess of the award amounts, and because to do so was seen to enhance the leverage the graduate school had in fostering improvements in the ORI targeted disciplines.

Because a comprehensive educational approach requires persons with the leverage to effect system-wide change, the leadership of graduate deans and the support of other senior leaders are central to this effort. As the CGS 2006 monograph *Graduate Education in the Responsible Conduct of Research* states, graduate deans are among the most powerful agents of change in "advancing ethics education as the central factor shaping the ethical climates of their institutions. And graduate deans, as visible campus officers well-positioned to promote ethics education, can themselves influence the ethical climate, by playing leadership roles in promoting awareness of ethical issues and by deliberating them in public forums" (CGS, 2006, p.11).

Summary

In the PSI, graduate schools were instrumental in embedding each of these three design principles into their institution's projects. Graduate deans and other senior administrators set the tone for a "values-based" campus discussion about enhancements to graduate education in scholarly integrity. They also coordinated the administration and analysis of surveys, and led communications regarding the purposes of assessment and their results. Finally, they convened appropriate individuals and helped align campus units to ensure that the education students receive in the all-important student-advisor relationship reinforces, and is reinforced by, other "touch points" throughout the graduate student's program of study.

Chapter 3.
A Framework for
Collaborative Action

In the initial stages of the PSI, the planning committee for the project was charged to identify core components of a comprehensive, institutional approach to advancing research integrity through graduate education. The resulting PSI framework was generated to foster the development and assessment of programs that are: comprehensive (as opposed to piecemeal), collaborative (as opposed to dependent on any single campus unit), sustainable beyond the period of external funding and the championship of any single individual, and attentive to a range of needs and issues in the graduate community.

The five-part PSI framework that resulted was intended to be flexible enough to allow for innovation and institutional differences, but structured enough to facilitate the mutual exchange of ideas and information among participating universities. It is premised on the notion that genuine, positive culture change at an institution involves effective leadership at all levels and at every stage. Through the PSI, graduate schools were to be encouraged to:

1. *Engage* the community in identifying needs,
2. *Invite* key stakeholders to reflect on a plan for action,
3. *Act* on those reflections (putting the plan into motion, implementation of project activities)
4. *Communicate* to the broader community about activities and their ongoing impact, and
5. *Integrate* activities to ensure greatest impact and sustainability.

This framework provided the structure for activities undertaken by the six awardee institutions.

These steps were outlined with the understanding that they did not represent a strict sequence and that feedback loops may occur at different points. For example, inviting faculty and campus leaders to brainstorm about issues and potential strategies for action may precede efforts to focus the attention of the broader community on the need for action, and may help to identify particular needs that will help to convince others of the importance of the project. Also, as both curricular and administrative integration are among the chief goals of this project, questions of integration and sustainability would need to be considered in the initial planning stages.

1. Engage the community in identifying needs.

The PSI approach brought together stakeholders from across the research and scholarly communities of participating campuses to define and reflect upon their programs as they evolve. The model programs and strategies that resulted, and that are the focus of this book, are examples of how strong graduate school leaders can catalyze leadership at all levels (faculty, staff, and students) to enhance the quality of graduate education and the institutional climate for integrity in research and scholarship.

The planning committee recognized two different approaches to focusing the graduate community's attention on the need for a more systematic approach to research ethics and integrity and for garnering broad campus support, at least in the early phases of the campus projects. The two approaches were recommended both for adoption by CGS in communicating the aims of the project and for consideration by graduate deans as they develop comprehensive strategies to integrate research and scholarly integrity into the fabric of graduate education at their universities. They could be adopted simultaneously or could provide alternatives for securing buy-in among different potential collaborators and constituencies. It was recognized that different leadership styles and different institutional cultures may encourage senior administrators to place differing emphases on each approach in their overall strategies, but also that no approach should overemphasize compliance to the exclusion of values-based discussions and activities. Regardless of the emphasis, true inroads into the culture of scholarship and research behavior were seen to require a broader recognition of the essential role that integrity plays in the definition of scholarship.

Recognizing vulnerabilities

The first approach recommended was for graduate schools to promote broad recognition of "vulnerabilities" and link these vulnerabilities to opportunities for enhanced graduate education in research integrity. Graduate schools are positioned to send a powerful message about how and where individuals, institutions, and the research enterprise are vulnerable. This does not simply mean inducing anxiety or fear about the possible consequences of error, misconduct, or misbehavior. It does mean prompting others to recognize that, as members in a community of researchers and as institutions, we are not doing enough to develop students as responsible members of their profession and to keep students and faculty up to date; to empower students as ethical agents; to encourage reflection in the disciplines and across the university about what concepts such as integrity and responsible conduct entail; and to incite innovative ideas about what education resources would best reinforce those concepts.

Possible activities recommended for consideration in proposals included:

- Establish the local context(s). There are various levels to the institutional context for scholarship: e.g., the course, the study group, the lab, the institution, and the discipline. These should be defined and understood as potential fields for activity.

    o Conduct focus groups, visits, and surveys to understand perceptions of students, faculty, and administration and compare their perceived scope of instruction, efficacy of instruction, and overall level of research integrity in the campus climate.
    o Analyze results for gaps and use any gap data to build recognition of disparities (e.g., between graduate teaching goals and graduate learning).
    o Share findings with the community through publication and focused discussion.

- Create greater transparency and "public forums" about the issues, capitalizing where possible on incidents that may arise.
- Evaluate and review policies and their implementation.
- Promote "difficult discussions" in curricula, in workshops, and in public forums. (Both students and faculty should be involved in these discussions.) Examples include: the obligations and risks of whistleblowing, the ownership of dissertation data, and the ethics of risk management and innovation vs. risk-avoidance in ethical deliberation.
- Emphasize the importance of ongoing professional development for faculty as well as students.

Recognizing excellence in research and education

The second approach recommended was to reward excellence in fostering research integrity and the responsible conduct of research. Recognition and rewards provided a way for graduate schools to emphasize that the university values these qualities in researchers, faculty, and students. The planning committee felt strongly, based on their combined experiences in leading graduate reform efforts and research integrity programs, that a rewards and values approach could be as effective as an approach that emphasizes vulnerabilities in gaining buy-in from research faculty. This is especially the case where there may be skepticism about the need for greater attention to the issues or if there is a feeling that addressing them implies ethical shortcomings of researchers or their students. An emphasis on the highest ideals and standards of the profession, including educational and mentoring standards, should be re-enforced where appropriate through a model that emphasizes rewards and recognition rather than simply the potential consequences of misconduct. An approach that recognizes excellence could be especially influential, committee members noted, if it emphasized the positive importance of senior researchers as examples.

Possible activities that build on this approach included:

- Awards celebrating individual mentors recognized for outstanding contributions to advancing the ethical and responsible conduct of research.
- Block grants to programs to recognize innovative approaches.
- Face-to-face "Socratic" dialogues, or issues-based case studies and vignettes.
- Building mentoring into tenure and promotion processes.
- Recognition of professional ethics as a critical element in the tenure and promotion process.
- Integration with existing programs that have both credibility and scope, such as "Preparing Future Faculty" or "Preparing Future Professionals" programs.

2. Invite campus stakeholders to reflect on a plan of action.

The second action step is to convene and to invite and incite reflection of key faculty members (especially those thought leaders who have the potential to serve as future change agents), staff, and students on how best to address the university's needs and vulnerabilities.

Possible actions recommended for consideration included:

- Solicit a clear, public endorsement of this project's goals by the university president or provost.
- Appoint a planning or steering committee (see CGS, 2006).
- Appoint a project director, where appropriate.
- Create a forum that can be perceived as a neutral place where everyone's positions can be valued.

3. Put the plan into motion/Implement project activities.

Under the leadership of the graduate dean or institutional equivalent, design and follow through on a plan for action will require making determinations and taking action in the areas of:

a) Content
b) Sequencing of Content and Pedagogy
c) Collaboration
d) Assessment

Content

Universities participating in the PSI gave careful consideration to whether they could adapt existing curricular materials to meet their needs or whether they needed to create new curricular content. Where creating new materials, key stakeholders were expected to have input into identifying the shortcomings of existing materials, and suggest concrete areas for improvement. If projects required adopting and/or adapting existing resources, a clear rationale for choices of curricular content was required. If new materials were needed, a clear plan with potential collaborators identified and resources available was to be established in advance.

One of the core features of the PSI was to encourage approaches that embed, in a rich curriculum, education in each of the core areas of responsible conduct of research as identified below. Activities and resources were expected to address the professional standards pertaining to these areas, as well as the bedrock principles and values behind them:

1) Data Acquisition, Management, Sharing, and Ownership
2) Conflicts of Interest and Commitment
3) Human Subjects
4) Animal Welfare
5) Research Misconduct
6) Publication Practices and Responsible Authorship
7) Mentor and Trainee Responsibilities
8) Peer Review
9) Collaborative Research

Other areas that were recommended for consideration in a comprehensive approach included:

Lab management
Classroom management and practice
Financial stewardship
Ethical decision-making and deliberation processes
Ethical principles
Hazardous Materials

Under "classroom management and practice," for example, some members of the planning committee noted that that the "term paper" is often less clearly defined than published papers in campus RCR programs, but issues of integrity and the ethics of authorship are equally germane here. The classroom can also provide an optimal space for learning about issues such as data management and authorship in a non-threatening environment, i.e., where the criteria for "sanctionable" offenses and consequences may be less severe and less public.

Sequencing of Content and Pedagogy

Institutions considering an integrative, comprehensive approach to research integrity should give thought to how content will be sequenced: i.e., how content, activities, and resources will address developmental needs of students at appropriate stages in their graduate path. Through the PSI website (www.scholarlyintegrity.org), CGS directs attention to available online resources and resources on best practices in content and delivery, and through the PSI encouraged innovation where appropriate in the development of curricular content.[13]

Whether institutions proposed to develop original curricular content or to innovate in the area of pedagogy and learning, they were asked to articulate how proposed activities were grounded in theories of learning. Projects were required to take advantage of the pedagogical context of graduate education to go beyond minimal training in proper conduct and professional standards. For example, universities could explore the pedagogical opportunities in hosting "difficult discussions" in workshops or other settings, and/or prepare students and faculty for professional situations that do not have easy right and wrong solutions but may instead require them to consider multiple, competing interests and hierarchies of value.

The inclusion of face to face <u>and</u> interactive learning opportunities was required as an essential characteristic of instruction in the PSI. Additional elements could include:

- An active writing journal, integrated into courses, that might include reflection on incidents that occur where issues of research ethics and responsible conduct arise, and mentoring on the more self-reflective aspects of research practice.
- Online interactive, or other technology that engages interaction,
- Passive web or published printed materials

Possible activities recommended for consideration included:

- Adaptation of existing online passive or interactive curricular materials to a face to face workshop or classroom context.
- Development of courses or content that escalate in complexity, e.g. via decision trees.
- Development of a "teachable moments" model across the curriculum, with workshops for faculty that focus on how to recognize teachable moments.
- Workshops that provide an open forum for students and faculty to tackle "difficult discussions."
- The inclusion of research ethics and integrity discussions in orientation.
- Re-evaluation of the role of education for research integrity in existing course offerings or degree requirements.

---

13. Some of the existing resources are now available through the ORI website (http://ori.dhhs. gov/) and the dedicated PSI website (www.scholarlyintegrity.org).

Collaboration

This PSI required collaboration among key stakeholders from across the participants' institutions. Universities planning such an approach to research integrity were encouraged to ask themselves: Who must be involved in order to fully scale up graduate education for research integrity? Who should or could be involved as potential collaborators? Suggestions included:

- President or provost, from whom support is essential
- Senior research officer, where appropriate, e.g., Senior VP for Research, from whom support is also essential
- Academic deans
- Graduate Council
- Center for instructional development and research
- Faculty council and subcommittee that works on instructional quality and subcommittee on professional standards. (The comment was made that faculty leading in these efforts are not necessarily graduate faculty but may be "mapped onto other structures.")
- Faculty
- Office of educational assessment
- Student organizations
- Postdoctoral fellows and/or students
- Student Affairs
- Ombudsperson

Assessment

A multi-tiered assessment approach is important for ensuring comprehensive and effective implementation. Institutions seeking to take a comprehensive approach to integrating research ethics and research integrity into graduate education were asked to consider at least three types of assessment:

Program implementation

CGS developed a set of instruments that universities participating in the Project or Scholarly Integrity were asked to use to assess the development of activities. The assessment instrument (consisting of pre- and post-implementation surveys) sought to gain understanding of the scope, impact, integration, visibility, and potential sustainability of funded projects.

The culture or climate for scholarly integrity

CGS helped facilitate consultation between subject and assessment experts and participating project PI's to adopt an assessment instrument (Thrush et al. 2006; Thrush, Martinson, Crain, & Wells, 2011) to measure the extent to which perceptions reflect improvements in the campus culture or climate of research integrity.[14]

Student learning

Universities participating in the Project for Scholarly Integrity developed or adapted instruments for assessing student learning and were encouraged to share these instruments with each other and with the CGS community. [To inform this activity, CGS provided information on the project website about student learning assessment tools developed as a result of prior CGS RCR initiatives and other, e.g. ORI-funded, initiatives.]

In assessment areas i and ii, CGS asked universities participating in the Project for Scholarly Integrity to engage in pre-implementation and to commit to post-implementation assessment. Ongoing assessment activities were encouraged: (1) to ensure that proposed activities reflected an understanding of the campus climate and existing programmatic resources, and (2) to measure change over time fostered by the project funding. Universities engaged in these three areas of assessment were asked to plan opportunities to reflect on the relationship (and any potential discrepancies) between the findings of these respective assessment instruments.

4. Communicate to the broader community about activities and their ongoing impact.

Communication or dissemination to the broader community, including communication about activities and their ongoing impact, is an important activity for ensuring the success of efforts led by the graduate school. Graduate schools were asked to encourage stakeholders to take advantage of appropriate venues, and should create new ones where appropriate, for sharing information

---

14. The CGS 2006 monograph *Graduate Education for the Responsible Conduct of Research* states: "Though the term 'ethical climate' may lack precision, graduate deans can contribute to the usefulness of the notion by insisting on the development of assessment instruments to define and measure it" (p. 11).

about administrative and process innovations as well as resources and instruments with each other and with the broader community. CGS also encouraged senior administrators and project directors to help each other improve existing resources in conjunction with partnering universities. Participants in the project were asked to address how any instruments created or processes developed that prove to be effective or promising would be shared with other universities. As part of the Project for Scholarly Integrity, CGS developed an electronic and communication infrastructure for regular exchange of ideas, and universities were encouraged to share their results with the broader community through meetings and publications.

5. Integrate activities to ensure greatest impact and sustainability.

One of the key assumptions of the PSI was that a sustainable comprehensive approach to research integrity requires the thoughtful integration and alignment of various components that can only be undertaken under the direction of senior leadership. This requires activities focused on two sets of considerations:

a) Aligning Curricular Activities, Administrative Structures, and Policies and Procedures Curricular Integration

Universities were asked to include a plan for integrating existing curricular resources (whether these are "homegrown" or include other, publicly available resources) into the fabric of graduate education on campus (e.g. via workshops, face to face seminars, assessment, etc.). This could entail both curricular integration and administrative integration. For example, the graduate school may leverage resources to encourage that a successful course or workshop offered in one discipline is adapted to meet the needs of another discipline, or that a course that effectively but sporadically addresses research ethics issues championed by one professor in one program may be offered on a more permanent basis, possibly taught by alternate faculty. The development of curricular materials can focus the energies of faculty and students and staff who may contribute to the development of content, even from across disciplines (as happens in the development of video vignettes depicting case studies, for example). Alternative activities may include: adapting resources developed elsewhere to one's own institutional needs; the scaling up of curricular content from a small population to a larger one; and the transferability of content from one discipline to another are important routes to developing a comprehensive approach.

Administrative structures

Existing administrative and educational structures can serve as important resources and conduits for the project's activities. Such resources may include: IRB offices, research administration staff, professional development programs, etc. Universities should consider which resources are the most likely partners in the short term, where there may be immediate buy-in, and which may be good partners in the longer term, where relationships may need to be cultivated.

Policies and Procedures

In developing the framework, the planning committee discussed the high probability that universities seeking to fully embed research ethics into graduate curricula would benefit from reinforcing that commitment through a simultaneous review of institutional processes and procedures. Universities and degree programs should ask how university-wide and program policies and procedures interact with individual decisions and behaviors in of the content areas identified above. In planning to develop a comprehensive approach to research ethics, universities were encouraged to identify areas where improvements upon current interactions are needed and possible mechanisms for improvement.

Possible activities recommended included:

- Review rules for funding research.
- Require investigators, as part of the process of submitting to an institutional review board, "a sixth chapter" that analyzes ethical issues raised by the research and/or its application, and specifies what alternatives were considered?
- Review application of procedures for response to misconduct allegations.

b) Sustainability, Transferability, and Scalability

Universities participating in the CGS Project for Scholarly Integrity were also asked to provide evidence that the activities supported by this project are sustainable beyond the expiration of external project funds, that they are replicable or transferable to other universities, and that thought has been given to what elements may and may not be readily adapted by other universities, and that, more generally, the activities are scalable, or can be adapted to institutions with larger or smaller populations, as appropriate.

Questions that universities should consider include:

How will one resource, instrument, or set of resources and instruments be integrated with other existing resources and tools to obtain maximal leverage and impact? How will activities be sustained over time? How will curricular activities undertaken be made known and content made accessible to other universities?

Conclusion

While the PSI framework provided institutions with a common structure for their activities, and some common activities and assessment strategies, all participants shaped their programs in a way that reflected unique characteristics of their campus and mission. The six universities in the PSI include both public and private institutions, with different strengths in terms of fields of concentration and mission. Their projects reflected those differences and reflected the fact that they began at different stages in the development of research integrity programs. All of the universities in the PSI were doctoral universities with significant research funding, however, and similarities between these institutions may mean that not all of the promising practices identified here will be feasible for every CGS member institution. Many of the activities sponsored by PSI project institutions included master's as well as doctoral students. But some activities and strategies described here may not be feasible for colleges or smaller, master's-focused institutions with limited staff and resources (for a preliminary discussion of scaling RCR programs for master's institutions, see CGS, 2009). Part II describes how the PSI institutions used the framework provided above to develop comprehensive programs and the lessons learned in implementing these programs.

PART II

Promising Practices: Lessons from Six Model Programs

Chapter 4.
PSI Project Profiles

E ach university in the Project for Scholarly Integrity carried out a set of activities and interventions unique to their institutions. In all cases, these activities were designed by each to advance the quality of research integrity and RCR programs for graduate students already in discussion or in place. The profiles below describe the activities of each PSI project as described on the PSI website (www.scholarlyintegrity.org) and updated based on institutions' final reports, which are included as Appendix C.

Columbia University

The Columbia University Graduate School of Arts and Sciences (GSAS) built upon existing programs in Responsible Conduct of Research (RCR) training and developed new activities and initiatives. The program solicited and addressed the specific reported needs of Columbia's Ph.D. students, which vary both according to discipline and to differences in preparation for the graduate research experience. An important goal of the program was the development of a carefully sequenced, and interactive, pedagogy surrounding RCR training, one that builds in complexity over the course of a Ph.D. candidate's training. With the aim of disseminating program results to other institutions, Columbia worked with other research institutions in the Inter-University Doctoral Consortium (IUDC) to participate in activities such as workshops and speaker series presentations.

Seven new initiatives were developed in the project:

- Appointment of **Research Ethics Fellows,** a total of 24 Ph.D. students across disciplines, who are responsible for administering program-specific activities and assessments. Each Research Ethics Fellow is designated a Research Ethics Faculty Mentor to advise him or her on program- and discipline-specific issues.

- Creation of a **Research Ethics Speaker Series** whereby faculty and Ph.D. students will submit proposals to host a scholar from their discipline who will address research ethics issues for the field.
- Revamping of an existing **graduate course** to emphasize RCR issues.
- Development of a **new course** focusing on RCR issues in the social sciences and humanities.*
- Development of an **RCR and Scholarly Integrity website** with a target audience of graduate students. The site was posted on the GSAS home page with links to existing Columbia and other institutional and governmental resources, codes of professional ethics in the disciplines, and best RCR practices from Columbia's Ph.D. programs.
- Expansion of the **Preparing Future Faculty** program.*
- Addition of a 60 minute break-out session to **new student orientation**.*

Approximate Number of Direct PSI participants:
728 students, 59 faculty DGS's + 18 additional faculty

Program Assessment respondents:
29 programs

Campus Partners:
Graduate School, Compliance Office, Teaching Center, faculty, students

Most Successful Activities:
Needs assessment/open forum discussions (students and postdocs); Advisory Board meeting (RCR expert faculty and program/college faculty)

Emory University

Emory University used PSI participation to develop a process-oriented program in research ethics and integrity, one that pays close attention to the unique pedagogical challenges of RCR awareness and training. In particular, Emory sought to build contexts in which ethical dilemmas can be candidly discussed, since evidence suggests that many students fear judgment in addressing ethical problems in research. The program was also process-oriented in the

---

* Initiatives marked with an asterisk were based on existing programs and were not developed with PSI funds.

sense that it focused on a student's development as a responsible researcher, and supported that development with three distinct goals. The first, **program integration**, was based on the principle that education in research ethics and integrity must be integrated into the curriculum of the student's program. Second, Emory worked to **hone students' skills of critical reflection** on the complicated problems of professional integrity. Third, the program **developed students' knowledge of research principles** established by the law, professional codes of ethics, and best practices in the discipline. Guided by these goals, this program sought to construct a systematic program of education in research ethics and integrity to be implemented across the Graduate School.

In addition to the three central ideas, three overlapping phases were intended to develop content and structure in response to perceived needs of the faculty and graduate students, and to build community consensus around the final product.

In phase one, focusing on **community vulnerabilities and opportunities**, Emory raised awareness about ethical issues. In phase two, **curricular capacity development,** Emory introduced courses or course content addressing the vulnerabilities specific to a discipline, research area, or methodology; introduced courses and workshops to be given at the Graduate School level; and developed faculty capacity to effectively teach the courses at both the program and school levels. In phase three, **implementation,** Emory developed course content that responded to needs not currently met; introduced graduate courses and workshops that respond to university-wide needs; and trained a cadre of faculty in RCR pedagogy.

Approximate Number of Direct PSI participants:
200 students, 130 faculty, 20 staff

Program Assessment respondents:
37 programs

Campus Partners:
Graduate School, faculty, Ethics Center

Most Successful Activities:
Speaker series and multi-disciplinary program; working group to review Emory's activities, identify gaps, and consider other institutions' best practices

Website:
http://www.graduateschool.emory.edu/resources/professional.php?entity_id=199

Michigan State University, Pennsylvania State University, and the University of Wisconsin-Madison

MSU, PSU, and UW-M worked collaboratively to jointly assess the research integrity "climate" in behavioral and biological sciences at their respective institutions. Since each institution has already worked with its respective faculty governance organization on elements of the individual campus action plans related to RCR, these committees were consulted as stakeholders and engaged in evaluating appropriate policy changes. Honoring the long history of partnership among the universities, the three institutions worked together to improve the climate for scholarly integrity and to assess the outcomes of RCR activities. In addition, each university individually undertook new institution-specific projects.

The multi-campus portion of the project included two components:

- First, all schools completed an initial **CGS inventory assessment**, a survey to assess the research integrity policies, practices, and resources. A later survey of activities and assessment survey documented institutional changes and impacts as the basis for individual and collective evaluation of results.
- Second, all schools completed a survey of organizational research climate created for this project and based on a survey developed by Carol Thrush and Brian Martinson (2011).

The institution-specific projects are detailed below:

Michigan State University conducted an analysis of graduate student handbooks regarding the section, "Departmental Policies: Integrity and Safety in Research and Creative Activities." The Research Integrity Council developed a "Needs Statement" for affirmative education in responsible conduct in research and creative activities.

Pennsylvania State University used the project to move forward on a new requirement for RCR education for all graduate students. Colleges were responsible for developing and delivering discussion-based, discipline-specific RCR education to their respective graduate students. The College of Health and Human Development acted as an experimental group in which faculty were required to deliver a systematically designed RCR program to graduate students. The faculty designated to lead the HHD program participated in workshops to learn the fundamentals about teaching research integrity to graduate students prior to leading the programs. PSU sought to assess the learning outcomes of the

HHD students in comparison to randomly selected students who participate in less systematic RCR programs offered by other colleges. PSU also established an advisory panel, made campus visits to collaborating institutions, and organized two forums to launch and then present the results of the project.

University of Wisconsin-Madison developed a graduate student-mentor compact program and incorporated scholarly integrity and professional standards into a campus-wide future faculty preparation program.

Program Assessment respondents:
MSU: 16 programs reported
PSU: 75 programs

Campus Partners:
MSU: Graduate School, MSU Research Integrity Council, Research Integrity Officer, college deans
PSU: Graduate School, college deans, Survey Research Center, Office of Research Protections

Most Successful Activities:
MSU: Survey implementation, Data analysis and discussions
PSU: "Train the trainers" faculty workshops (participation spread beyond HHD, senior faculty engaged)

Websites:
MSU: http://www.vprgs.msu.edu/climate_survey;
PSU: http://www.research.psu.edu/training/sari/

University of Alabama at Birmingham

While in the past, Responsible Conduct of Research (RCR) and Scholarly Integrity (SI) were taught within a single required graduate course at The University of Alabama at Birmingham, UAB used the Project for Scholarly Integrity to give students periodic and consistent opportunities to develop skills for responsible research. The program's focus on embedded skills also alleviated the time burden on researchers who face the pressure to secure renewal of extramural funding. By developing a program that was fully integrated into graduate training, UAB sought to make it easier for students and faculty to frequently and openly discuss research ethics. The theoretical framework for assessing SI activities is the Trilogy Model, which is guided by three principles for producing lasting change: Engagement, Capacity, and Continuity. Each of the following activities involved one or more of the components, and were evaluated over the course of the program:

- Surveying graduate students' perceptions of education in scholarly integrity issues and identifying perceived "vulnerabilities."
- Upholding, promoting, and administering at a formal ceremony a student oath to maintain high standards of scholarly integrity.
- Developing new workshops on topics related to scholarly integrity, including identifying topics for future workshops and targeting audiences for the workshops.
- Developing supporting videos for workshops and small group sessions, including "decision tree" videos that dramatize ethical dilemmas.
- Developing online materials for use in small group meetings and targeting audiences for use of online materials.
- Using TA training as an opportunity to teach scholarly integrity issues.

Approximate Number of Direct PSI participants:
700 graduate students, 75+ undergraduates, 55 to 90 faculty

Program Assessment respondents:
39 programs

Campus Partners:
Graduate School, Ethics Center, Compliance Office, Institutional Research, Center for Clinical and Translational Science

Most Successful Activities:
Ethical Authorship workshops, Embedding RCR Education into TA Training; Online Videos to prompt student discussions

Website:
http://www.uab.edu/graduate/researcg/project-for-scholarly-integrity

The University of Arizona

The University of Arizona used participation in the Project for Scholarly Integrity to integrate graduate students' individualized and discipline-specific activities into a comprehensive program in RCR. More specifically, they joined RCR curriculum development in individual departments to campus-wide discussions and special events, and keyed individual or lab-based curricula to the larger goals of RCR training. The program's new activities, which both developed and implemented new RCR policies, allowed students and faculty to play a role in decision-making and policy implementation. With these new strategies, Arizona aimed to meet the particularly complex research issues emerging in developing disciplines, including space exploration, optical sciences, and anthropology, as well as biomedicine and behavioral health, water and energy sustainability, and Native, Latin American, and Borderlands studies.

Arizona used five interrelated PSI activities to increase awareness of research integrity:

- A university-wide **Research Integrity Days Conference,** which includes workshops in research integrity issues conducted by national and international leaders. This high-profile, public event demonstrates to the community that research integrity issues are central to the mission of the university.
- A **Research Integrity Advisory Group** composed of junior faculty and graduate students engages the university administration in policy development and advises the Graduate College.
- A **Research Integrity Small Grants Program** funds curriculum development for full courses in RCR as well as modules that can be incorporated into existing science and methods courses. The small grants program encourages graduate students and junior faculty to think creatively about ways to engage their students in discussions about the responsible conduct of research.
- A **Graduate Certificate in Responsible Conduct of Research** provides a three-course series in RCR training for graduate students and postdocs.
- A **Research Integrity Resource Center**, housed in the newly created Office for the Responsible Conduct of Research, contains curricular materials gathered from Research Integrity Days and newly developed modules and courses.

Approximate Number of Direct PSI participants:
406 students, 200 faculty, 50 staff

Program Assessment respondents:
44 programs

Campus Partners:
Graduate School, RCR Office, UA Libraries, faculty, students

Most Successful Activities:
Small Grants in Research Integrity Program (and requirement for graduate students to partner with faculty members)

Website:
http://orcr.vpr.arizona.edu/RIconference

Chapter 5.
Engaging the Community in Identifying Needs

A t the outset of their projects, each of the six PSI institutions engaged various groups on campus to identify needs and gaps in graduate education for scholarly integrity and the responsible conduct of research. This step was as important for the message it sent as for the information it helped gather. By soliciting input from different groups and campus units, graduate deans and graduate schools sought to convey that research integrity was relevant to all members of the graduate community—faculty, graduate students, graduate administrators and staff.

The preceding section described the design principles and a framework for program design provided to participating universities as they planned their PSI projects. In this chapter and throughout Part II, the emphasis is on common practices shared by participants that suggest generalized principles applicable to most CGS member universities. Call-out boxes are interspersed throughout, however, to provide additional details on aspects of each project that were unique. These "Spotlights" focus on specific processes, activities, and resources institutions reported to be particularly effective or challenging at their institutions.

Two Basic Approaches to Engaging Campus Partners

As noted in the previous section, the PSI Framework Document that accompanied the RFP for this project outlined two distinct but mutually compatible approaches for graduate schools to use to engage the interest, support, and feedback of their communities on their PSI projects. The first was to create opportunities to *recognize vulnerabilities* as institutions and individuals and consider how institutions might better prepare graduate students to conduct research in a responsible and ethical manner; the second was to *reward excellence* to convey the positive values behind research and scholarly integrity.

The most common approaches taken to building recognition of vulnerabilities into the engagement plans of PSI institutions included[15]:

- Using surveys to assess needs, perceptions, and available resources;
- Raising awareness by sharing survey results and hosting "public forums" about research integrity issues;
- Evaluating and reviewing policies and their implementation;
- Promoting "difficult discussions" among faculty and students in curricula, workshops, and in public forums; and
- Emphasizing the importance of professional development for faculty as well as students.

In assessing needs and vulnerabilities, PSI graduate schools explored different ways of emphasizing the importance of compliance with policies and codes. On the one hand, all agreed that it was important to communicate that students, faculty, and the institution as a whole were placed at risk in an environment where there is uncertainty about or lack of respect for the rules. At the same time, there was also a need to stress that the consequences of noncompliance went well beyond those of "getting caught."

In project meetings, graduate deans discussed ways to position their projects in relationship to new NSF and NIH research training requirements. Initially, opinions were divided about the extent to which aligning university projects with new training requirements from funding agencies would reinforce or compromise the aims of the projects. As projects evolved, however, a consensus emerged that one great advantage of the new regulations is that they provided incentives for faculty to avail themselves of the resources and materials graduate schools were providing through the PSI. MSU, for example, incorporated survey results into a PowerPoint presentation to present across the campus in colleges and units on the recent NSF requirement for RCR training. The University of Arizona reported that "our CGS/ORI PSI project was instrumental in preparing us to "provide resources to campus in the culture of RCR and ethics rather than simply responding to the [NIH and NSF] mandates in a compliance mentality." Similarly, Columbia University reported that, "when Columbia's Office of Research, Division of Research Compliance Education [OR/RCE] began to identify existing resources at Columbia that would help

---

15. This step was recommended in CGS's Graduate Education and the Responsible Conduct of Research, 2006.

trainees meet the new NSF RCR training requirement, [it] found our RCR/PSI Activities Training Inventory to be the most comprehensive survey available of central, school, and departmental RCR training."

In taking the second approach, to *reward excellence*, PSI institutions built into their engagement plans a number of the strategies from the PSI Framework Document described earlier in Part I. These included:

- Block grants to programs to develop innovative approaches to curricular development;
- Integration of research integrity education into the faculty reward and recognition processes, including awards that specifically recognized strong mentoring in research integrity; and
- Integration of research integrity into existing professional development programs such as Preparing Future Faculty and similar programs. Sections B and C, below, provide more detailed information about implementation of these approaches at PSI institutions.

Participants noted that faculty participation in research integrity education of graduate students may be indirectly credited in tenure and promotion processes, at least in some fields, to the extent that compliance with federal guidelines for research integrity may affect the success of some faculty members in securing research funding. Institutions also discussed mechanisms for recognizing faculty excellence in this area within more generic criteria for evaluation, such as demonstrated accomplishments in teaching and mentoring.

Effective Communication Strategies

As PSI participants began to identify areas where focused work was needed, they also began to implement specific communication strategies for their projects. Some universities acknowledged that they initially underestimated the importance of shaping an effective communication strategy to cut through the noise of, as one university dubbed it, "memo overload." Across the project, three communication strategies were found to be particularly effective:

- Connecting PSI goals with existing professional and scholarly norms
- Presenting content in an academic, intellectual context
- Conveying how PSI content is relevant to specific subunits (disciplinary units or programs, and other institutional contexts for research)

1. Connecting PSI with Professional Norms

One of the first questions that universities faced was how to develop effective messages about research integrity that were perceived as meaningful and relevant to the educational, scholarly and professional experiences of different groups on campus. Each graduate school worked to establish a balance between articulating positive values related to scholarly and research integrity and underlining the importance of compliance with policies and codes, looking for the right time and place to emphasize each.

All university partners set out to link their projects to values that were distinctive of their institutions and communities. Some began by examining the university's explicit values statements and touchstone documents, such as the university mission statement and graduate school website. Building upon these messages helped to align what might be seen as a new or unfamiliar project with the university's grounding values and activities.

As universities developed various strategies for communication, one particularly notable lesson emerged: messages about research integrity were most effective, they reported, when linked to professional and scholarly norms, practices and attitudes. This approach helped to distinguish graduate education for the responsible conduct of research from research integrity education at the undergraduate level, where the emphasis is often more narrowly focused on the importance of avoiding plagiarism and on learning responsible citation. An emphasis on professional norms conveys that, while these issues are still relevant to graduate preparation, responsible research practices go *beyond* what is expected of undergraduate preparation, and that both general and discipline-specific skills must be learned and honed throughout a graduate student's development as a scholar and researcher.

A focus on the education of professional researchers also helped graduate schools to preempt common objections to research integrity education based on common misperceptions. Such misperceptions include that education in research integrity is simply a form of moral education for potential wrongdoers or "bad apples," or that graduate students have learned, or should have learned, all they need to know about research integrity in their prior experiences as successful undergraduates in their field. The University of Alabama at Birmingham provides a good example of how issues can be re-branded in a way that resonates with graduate education:

> We needed effective marketing to engage students. To call
> the workshop "Avoiding Plagiarism" deterred some students.
> We rebranded it as "Ethical Authorship: Joining the Scholarly

Conversation" and emphasized effective and efficient writing strategies that would result in a lower likelihood of plagiarism, but also increased professional integrity and productivity. That changed the student perception of the activities from punitive ("Here's what will happen to you if you plagiarize.") to proactive ("Here's how I will improve my writing and note-taking skills, so I don't have to worry about plagiarism.")

Even when the curricular content remains the same, simply re-branding to more accurately describe what is being addressed, and doing so in a way that conveys the professional aspirations to quality research, can help to increase graduate student participation and faculty support.

2. Presenting PSI Content in an Academic Context

To create messages that would resonate with the graduate community, some institutions emphasized "higher order" professional and scholarly skills as well as research excellence. Below we highlight a number of ways in which universities defined and expressed these aspirational values to their communities.

Highlighting Research Quality and the Characteristics of Successful Researchers— Michigan State University (MSU)

MSU enlisted the support of the Provost and Vice President for Research, who wrote a letter to the entire graduate community linking the value of the PSI project to research quality. The message was consistent with the graduate school's earlier efforts to promote research integrity as a responsibility to a variety of stakeholders invested in the practice and impacts of research. MSU's graduate dean explained, "For us, this language explicitly focuses on the expectation of 'responsibility' to students, colleagues, and funders for quality research."

The graduate school also chose to translate the nine core areas of RCR into a set of positive values and professional attitudes that were communicated through a poster series. MSU's Research Integrity Council invited graduate students to participate in focus groups to recommend language

---

and images likely to catch the attention of graduate students and faculty. The values included honesty, recognition of others' work, confidentiality and respect for intellectual property, disclosure of potential conflicts of interest, compliance, protection of research participants, collegiality, and communication. To tie these values back to MSU research, the messages were accompanied by photographs of MSU students and faculty engaged in research activities.

MSU Checklist for Campus-Wide Communications:
- ✓ **Enlist the support of senior leadership.**
- ✓ **Solicit feedback on the message from students or faculty.**
- ✓ **Identify the positive or ideal characteristics of researchers.**
- ✓ **Link the initiative to real researchers on campus.**

The MSU example demonstrates a series of effective strategies for communicating that core areas of RCR are about professional formation rather than compliance. The graduate school conveys to all faculty that research integrity is integral, rather than peripheral, to quality research.

A contrasting example of an approach that links professionalization and research integrity can be found in Emory University's project. In addition to emphasizing core areas of RCR education, Emory gave special emphasis to skills of ethical deliberation, defined in their proposal as the ability to engage in "critical reflection on the complicated problems of research integrity." One program, reported as particularly successful, was a series of public forums on complex ethical issues in research that provided students and faculty with the opportunity to discuss ethical decision-making in research.

**Building an Intellectual Community around
Research Ethics– Emory University**

The series, "Beyond Right and Wrong: Engaging Ethics at Emory" featured well-known speakers on issues of research integrity and multidisciplinary discussion panels composed of faculty, researchers and students. Some of these lectures highlighted core areas of RCR (such as misconduct and animal welfare), but took these categories of training beyond the realm of compliance. The program stressed that professional scholars have complex and differing views on ethical issues in scholarship, problems that require well-honed critical thinking skills informed by knowledge. Following two of these public lectures, the graduate school hosted "town-hall" meetings with faculty, staff and graduate students to gather insights that could help shape future programming.

Emory Checklist for Campus-Wide Communications:
- ✓ **Create a forum for structured debate on a specific topic.**
- ✓ **Choose an academic format, i.e., a workshop or symposium**
- ✓ **Invite students and faculty to lead the discussion.**
- ✓ **Convey that research ethics is difficult, even for experts and seasoned researchers.**

The Emory program was conducted in a recognizably "academic" format—a lecture by a researcher followed by a panel discussion. This format helped reinforce the message that research integrity is worthy of high-level academic discussion and debate.

3. Conveying Relevance of PSI Content to Specific Subunits

Campus-wide communication efforts raise the question of how best to speak to programs and disciplines with different cultures of research and scholarship. Most of the PSI partners grappled with this issue. For example, Columbia University reported that some activities and communication efforts were "too general or generic to capture specific audiences" and recommended a combination of general and audience-specific communication strategies. Columbia found that student feedback contained helpful advice about how to "brand" PSI activities in ways that are perceived as relevant to target disciplines:

> We were intrigued by students' response to our central programming: Some students in the humanities thought the programming was too science-focused; some students in the sciences perceived the very same programming as more focused on the humanities. We learned that students want the workshop and discussion topics to be very focused on the specific circumstances they find themselves in. Several students told

us: "Don't use the term 'ethics' in your workshop titles; that is too generic. We won't come to workshops about ethics!" Instead they see their time better spent at events that help them solve the problems they were having with their advisors: how to talk to advisors who had not explained the lab's authorship policy or how to address concerns when faculty ask students to provide peer review of manuscripts without offering guidance or training and without acknowledging the work of the students. Students want just-in-time information . . . to help them with immediate dilemmas so they can return to the lab and to the library as quickly as possible.

One generally effective approach to tailoring messages to different disciplinary groups was to enlist the support of strong advocates within specific disciplines and fields. At larger institutions such as MSU and PSU, senior administrators with oversight for specific fields, such as college deans, were enlisted by the graduate school to communicate the value of the project within their particular school or college. And at small and large institutions alike, PSI partners reported, faculty champions played a critical role in communicating the value of research and scholarly integrity within their own disciplines and department. Ensuring that the project team include faculty members from multiple disciplines was essential. PSU reported, for example, that "allowing academic colleges to develop RCR programs that are specifically designed to address the issues within their disciplines was viewed as a critical component of implementing a successful university wide RCR initiative."

Chapter 6.
Inviting Campus Stakeholders to Reflect on a Plan of Action

The first area of promising practices discussed in the above chapter centers on what might be called communication strategy. This second area focuses on strategies to ensure participation and input from key faculty so that the goals of the graduate school and the programs and colleges are aligned from the outset.

Getting Organized

All PSI partners consulted a diverse range of campus stakeholders as they developed their proposals and planned the roll-out of major activities. For most, however, decision-making was an ongoing process that required a set of campus partners who could be consulted as the project developed. PSI awardees institutions implemented a number of strategies outlined in the PSI Framework Document, including:

- Appointing a planning or steering committee,
- Appointing a Project Director, and
- Creating a neutral forum for discussion and evaluation.

1. Steering Committees

Columbia, Emory, and the University of Alabama at Birmingham all chose to assemble steering committees that took on various tasks and responsibilities.

- Columbia created an Advisory Board that included graduate students, faculty, and administrators whose goal was to develop a campus-wide RCR program through monthly meetings.

- Emory University assembled a Steering Committee with the goal of developing a program that would be integrated into all doctoral programs. Because this program was to be required and needed to be relevant to different disciplines, they took care in assembling an interdisciplinary team of faculty and administrators that included representatives from the School of Medicine, the Emory Center for Ethics, and the Office of Research. Emory also assembled a "Program Working Group" tasked with generating ideas and feedback for the curricular content of the program.
- The University of Alabama at Birmingham's approach was more informal, reflecting a campus culture where communications often take place in person-to-person settings. The Dean's Office assembled a committee that included graduate students, faculty, staff, and administrators, consulting each group individually on issues that were most relevant to their interests or concerns.

In many cases these groups provided an environment for fostering student and faculty champions within programs. For example, Emory observed that faculty champions emerged from the Program Working Group. Early faculty involvement can also serve to build support for assessment efforts prior to the administration of surveys and the analysis and distribution of results. Awardees were agreed that a project that seeks to involve faculty in research integrity education should involve faculty from the start.

2. Project Directors

Appointing project liaisons and project directors was also found to be a successful strategy for a number of universities. At the University of Arizona, for example, where some activities resulted in enhancing and extending the impact of what was already being provided on a smaller scale, many of the project activities were planned by administrators who shared oversight for research compliance. This organizational structure posed a potential obstacle for achieving one of the main project goals, "to move research integrity out of the shelter of the compliance office and into the general culture of the university." To separate the project from compliance oversight, the Graduate College gave the coordinator of research integrity training programs the role of liaison between research administrators and students and faculty.

Creating leaders in the graduate school (or other central office) staff can also save time and ensure continuity and sustainability of the project. For example, one university saw significant changes in administrative personnel over the course of its project, which resulted in a period where new administrators had to be "brought up to speed" on past initiatives. The assistant dean who came into the project later in the initiative advised that staff leaders can "help with maintaining program continuity, allowing for continuous communication and progress with no break in activity."

Creating Partnerships and Alliances

Partnerships and alliances were critical to the success of individual projects. Partnerships provided expertise in areas that each graduate school needed to effectively lead their projects, opportunities for obtaining buy-in from different groups on campus, new mechanisms and venues for communicating the value of the project, and resources—including human resources—that could be leveraged to support the project goals. While the graduate school provided the core leadership for each of these projects, senior leadership of presidents, provosts, and college deans was also essential. As Columbia University reported, while their goal was to require RCR/SI [scholarly integrity] training for all Columbia Ph.D. students as a graduate school-wide requirement, "we would move forward only after having a comprehensive plan for shared leadership with the provost's office and the school deans."

Each of the graduate schools that participated in the PSI also had its own history of campus partnerships on which to build collaborative activities and alliances. Many also sought to create new partnerships or strengthen links with central campus units that had a vested interest in the outcomes of the project. The types of partnerships that PSI leaders used to enhance their projects were broad-ranging, and included a wide variety of stakeholders such as:

- Coordinators for Professional Development Programs for faculty and/or students, Student and Postdoctoral Associations,
- Ethics Centers,
- Research Offices,
- Research Integrity or Compliance Offices,
- Interdisciplinary Research Centers, and
- Graduate Student Associations.

PSI partners expressed that their most important partners for their projects were faculty in the program, but again, many these larger groups and alliances proved to be a good foundation for creating stronger relationships with faculty. The first case study in the next section, "Creating Buy-In for the Assessment Process," offers an interesting case in point.

Chapter 7.
Implementing Project
Activities

A s PSI awardees began to implement project activities, they met regularly with each other and CGS project staff to share challenges and lessons learned during various stages of the implementation process. Chapter 7 seeks to capture their observations during and after implementation of a range of educational initiatives for graduate students and faculty. Graduate deans provided important leadership in shaping the content of centrally delivered and program-based learning programs and ensuring that they had a broad impact across campus. Here we focus on three issues: developing the right content for programs, sequencing content and assuring the quality of pedagogy, and supporting effective collaborations.

Developing the Right Content

As explained in Chapter 3, all PSI awardees sought to develop resources that placed RCR in disciplinary contexts. Common approaches to developing content for programs included: engaging faculty in the process of creating or selecting content appropriate to RCR areas in the disciplines; engaging graduate students in developing such resources; and creating forums where graduate students and/or faculty could discuss the relevance of RCR issues to their own research.

One initiative that combined all of these approaches was a small grants program developed by the University of Arizona. The program offered individual graduate students or junior faculty small awards to develop innovative modules and courses that addressed core areas of RCR in their disciplinary areas. To cultivate interest in the grants, the project team held two informal meetings with faculty and graduate students who had expressed interest in the grant announcement. These meetings had a number of secondary benefits. The conversations with faculty and graduate students helped the Graduate College to identify key themes and integrity issues faced by graduate students within disciplines, information that was used to help shape the program for a high-profile conference on research integrity. It also helped the College to identify program advocates for its Research Integrity Advisory Group.

The RFP for the grants program led to a diverse range of proposals which included a series of introductory courses across the life sciences, a course addressing the challenges of research with Native American tribes, and a social sciences project on research using geospatial information. According to the project leaders, the program helped "offset a common obstacle to the development of programs—a lack of money and human resources." The text box below explains how the program design helped maximize the impact of individual awards.

Using Small Grants to Seed Campus-Wide Benefits
The University of Arizona

The University of Arizona's Small Grants in Research Integrity program shows how careful design of a grants program can lead to a number of indirect benefits. In the Request for Proposals, graduate students were required to partner with faculty mentors, which strengthened the dialogue between faculty and students about RCR and "provided opportunities for the direct application of RCR standards in mentoring, authorship, collaborative science, and research integrity." Participants in the program were also given the opportunity to be acknowledged for their work in a "Grantees Showcase" in the university's first annual campus-wide event on research integrity. This served not only to reward the accomplishments of students and faculty in RCR education, but also to support the professional development of graduate students who presented at the conference. Finally, grantees were asked to share the curricula they developed in an online repository of RCR resources for graduate students and faculty.

Participants in the grants program reported a number of other successful activities and outcomes that resulted from the program, including:

- Strong student interest in new courses, and the opportunity to pilot test modules with a highly engaged group;
- Opportunities to collaborate with other researchers and to identify new resources related to teaching research ethics;
- The ability to think beyond "standard" research protocol criteria; and
- The development of a new graduate seminar in RCR.

Yet another model for engaging students in RCR was developed by Columbia University: a series of lunch discussions for graduate students and postdocs that focused on issues of scholarly integrity and RCR. Although this program had a formal component—students could receive credit toward a training requirement in RCR—it also provided a more informal context for open discussion. A number of other universities that developed similar, neutral spaces for student discussion reported that such forums helped students discuss issues that they did not feel comfortable raising with their advisors. The goals and benefits of the program are described in greater detail in the text box below.

Engaging Students in Frank Discussions of Research Integrity
Columbia University

According to the project leaders at Columbia, one of the greatest benefits of their lunchtime series on research ethics and scholarly integrity was that it raised awareness about issues of research integrity that were often not addressed or reinforced in their departments or programs. The graduate school reported that the structured presentations for the series, followed by student discussions, often led to moments of revelation among students: "On many occasions and across several departments, student comments were met by this response from other students: 'I didn't know this was also an issue in your lab'; 'I have the same problem with my advisor.' 'Why have we not talked about this in the department before?'"

The focus of the seminars was professional development for graduate students and focused on topics of broad relevance to the disciplines. An additional benefit of the program is that it helped graduate students to become voices for change in their departments and work together to think pragmatically about addressing issues with their advisors. "The central programming was successful in that students from various disciplines discovered that they shared some of the same problems and concerns (e.g., about mentoring, authorship practices); on many occasions students shared solutions that worked in one program for possible use in another."

It is important to note that not all universities found small grants programs to be among the most successful PSI activities at their institutions. One university reported that it was difficult to generate sufficient student and faculty interest in submitting proposals. The project PI's reflected that there may be more interest in such a program now that their PSI project has achieved more visibility on campus, and they will consider re-advertising the grants at a later time.

Sequencing of Content and Pedagogy

PSI Awardee institutions also gave careful consideration to pedagogies appropriate to graduate education in scholarly integrity and RCR as well as to the sequencing of educational content. Two basic principles informed the development and implementation of most curricula: (1) the use of highly interactive methods of learning, and (2) attention to the phase of a graduate student's education (from first-year students, to those just beginning their dissertation work or teaching experiences, to those beginning to make transitions to academic and other professional positions).

Penn State University's Scholarship and Research Integrity (SARI) Program, described below, is an example of a project that offered graduate students multiple opportunities for learning about RCR and scholarly integrity issues at different stages of their graduate program. The SARI program was supplemented by a number of other voluntary programs that existed prior to the implementation of the project: a Research Integrity brownbag series developed to foster discussion of the nine core areas of RCR; Research Integrity Workshops provided annually to faculty and postdocs within each college; Survival Skills and Ethics workshops on professional skills related to ethics; and IRB workshops on human participant research.

**Implementing a Multi-Phase Graduate RCR Requirement
The Pennsylvania State University (PSU)**

The SARI program was launched in the first year of PSI implementation as a requirement for all graduate students entering the university in 2009. The program was designed to combine online and face-to-face instruction. During the first year of enrollment, graduate students are required to complete an online RCR training program focusing on core areas of RCR. In the early stages of implementation, PSU project staff reported that it was sometimes difficult to provide the same quality of online instruction across all fields, especially in the humanities, where fewer resources existed. The fact that the

---

SARI Program was led by a Director with oversight for the quality and consistency of the program made it possible to direct extra attention and effort to addressing this gap.

The second phase of the SARI program involves an additional five hours of discussion-based RCR education designed and provided by faculty in the disciplines. All graduate programs and Colleges were required to submit a plan to the Graduate School for providing this instruction. PSU reported that the face-to-face component of the program had the indirect benefit of getting faculty directly involved in RCR education and better prepared to integrate RCR issues into their own teaching. To support faculty who provided the face-to-face component of the program, the PSU project team organized formal training workshops and developed a website where all faculty could access pedagogical resources for graduate curricula on scholarly integrity and RCR.

In looking back on the development of the SARI program, PSU project leaders indicated that involving academic colleges in developing discipline-specific RCR programs was critical to the success of their program.

The University of Alabama at Birmingham's programs on RCR and scholarly integrity provide a useful point of contrast to the programming of a large state institution like PSU. UAB gave significant attention to researching and measuring the effectiveness of RCR pedagogies in a variety of different formats. Below we highlight two examples.

Workshops on Ethical Authorship

The UAB workshops were focused on an area of RCR that is relevant to all graduate programs and targeted to graduate students in their first and second years of study. Many different formats were used: video materials placed in the context of discussion activities, self-quizzes, interactive PowerPoint presentations, Case Studies, and writing activities, among others. Assessments of student learning enabled the instructors, two staff members in UAB's Graduate School Professional Development Program, to refine content and pedagogy. "We learned to develop many interactive short-duration activities [. . .] that could be assembled into workshops targeted at specific graduate student audiences." The graduate dean and associate graduate dean leading the project reported that the diversity of these activities will help them to emphasize faculty choice and judgment when sharing the resources with faculty: "As we roll these materials out to faculty champions, we want to emphasize the 'mix and match' nature of these activities, so different components can be assembled to match the needs of the target audience and the learning objective."

Embedding Ethics Education in the Training of Teaching Assistants

UAB integrated information about the pedagogies and content of RCR in a training course for TAs in the natural sciences and mathematics. The project was designed to help TAs understand and gain ownership of RCR issues by integrating them into their own lesson plans for undergraduate courses. As with Arizona's small grants program, giving graduate students an opportunity to be authorities on RCR with their own undergraduate students led to a high level of graduate student investment in RCR issues: "Students took this project very seriously, developing a creative mixture of materials for use, including short PowerPoint presentations, simulations, case studies, classroom quizzes, brochures, group discussions, and peer teaching and short lab experiments."

While all graduate deans may not be directly involved in the content of such programs prior to or during the implementation phase, they have an important role to play in a number of areas: asking questions about the alignment between a students' phase of study and the program delivered, ensuring that some form of quality assurance or learning assessment is part of these programs, and asking their project teams to build in features that will maximize benefits in areas such as mentoring, professional development for faculty, and outreach to other relevant campus units.

Building Collaborations

The programs described above have already demonstrated that strong relationships between different campus units play an important role in successful implementation of university activities. Not only did collaborations help the graduate school reach a larger number of students and faculty, including those who did not participate in formal activities, but they also provided opportunities for different units to become invested in the project outcomes. Project PIs indicated that one important aspect of successful collaboration was ensuring that project plans were flexible enough at the outset to integrate the suggestions of different stakeholders as well as make room for mid-course corrections. Sending the message that implementation is a dynamic process helped keep the lines of communication open between the graduate schools and many of their on-campus collaborators.

A number of universities also found that external collaborators significantly enhanced their projects and allowed them to draw from a broader range of resources and contributors. For example, Columbia University reported that some of their broader project activities were enriched by the participation of a number of graduate institutions in the New York City area. They also plan to extend these invitations as they seek to sustain their current activities by inviting other universities to jointly plan and host RCR and scholarly integrity activities. The project PIs remarked that this collaboration could be extended to other campuses via the internet, using listservs, web resources, and videos and Skype broadcasts of programming.

Finally, collaborations were essential in the area of assessment. Because assessment activities raise a number of specific issues and challenges, they are addressed in the next chapter, *Communication of Assessment Results*.

Chapter 8. Communicating the Purposes and Results of Assessment

Creating Buy-in for the Assessment Process

Assessment was a key component of the Project for Scholarly Integrity, as was the use of survey results to open conversations between graduate schools and programs about where the gaps were in curricula and what student needs remained unmet. A number of different assessment approaches were used, including surveys that are discussed at greater length in Part III. An integral assessment component to a research and scholarly integrity program can ground discussions between graduate schools and faculty in evidence about what resources and activities students are currently taking advantage of, how adequate faculty and students perceive these to be, and where there may be additional needs that are not being addressed through current education and training opportunities. Such discussions can also ensure that graduate schools are aware of what is already in place so duplication of effort can be avoided and so programs in need of models may be directed to peers with exemplary practices. Before convening program faculty to discuss survey results, for example the data from institutional climate and activities surveys, the graduate schools participating in the PSI recognized the need to first the support of faculty and other stakeholders (including graduate students) for the assessment goals and process.

Engaging Students in the Assessment Process: the University of Alabama at Birmingham

The University of Alabama at Birmingham used a "bottom-up" approach to creating buy-in for the climate assessment activities. UAB's graduate school already had strong relationships with a number of groups on campus, in particular, the Graduate Student Association and the representatives of specific graduate student organizations. At the outset of the project, the Associate Dean asked the Graduate Student Association for an invitation to attend one of their regular meetings and also met with the officers of the Postdoctoral Association about the climate survey assessments planned as part of the implementation stage of the project. The Associate Dean stressed the importance of understanding students' perceptions of the campus climate for research integrity, and also asked the students and postdocs for their feedback on the project. As a result of these meetings both associations spread the word about the importance of the climate assessment survey with members of their respective groups, likely increasing the response rate for students and postdocs who participated in the survey. Perhaps more surprisingly, however, this step proved important for creating buy-in for the survey with program *faculty* as well, because it demonstrated that interest in the survey was not only valued by the graduate school administration, but also by graduate students and postdoctoral fellows.

Frequent Communication and Follow-Up: the MSU, PSU, and University of Wisconsin-Madison Consortium

- Among the recommendations for effective assessment, the MSU/PSU/UWM consortium reported the following pertaining to communication and follow-up with key groups if you launch a climate survey as an assessment tool: Define and identify your desired sample populations: who participates in research? Be prepared to address results with each group.
- Seriously attend to notification and good will communications. These include leadership emails, newsletters (3-6 weeks prior to administration of

survey), and a knowledgeable and trusted person (e.g., the graduate dean) to answer every email question, phone call, or concern during the survey.
- Keep the vice provost for research (if separate from the graduate dean) and provost informed.
- Offer support, resources, and guidance from the Graduate School.
- Volunteer to work with individual units as they strive to improve their RCR climate.

The assessment data gathered through the PSI survey instruments and other needs assessment activities, such as focus group discussions and face-to-face meetings between graduate school staff and faculty, were used in a variety of ways. Analysis of assessment data may be used to identify and send a serious message to some campus units that either educational resources or climate are deficient or are not reaching their target audiences. The purposes of both the activities and the climate assessments (discussed in Part III), however, was primarily to identify areas of need and solicit input on optimal solutions. Several universities emphasized the importance of communicating the purposes of assessments relevant to graduate education for research integrity with departments and programs. Buy-in was more successfully obtained when it was clear that results would be used primarily to identify areas where the graduate school or other partner might assist campus units by either providing resources or directing faculty and program directors to appropriate sources of information in peer programs or on peer campuses about how to address those needs.

The PSI Activities Assessment Survey served multiple uses. The University of Arizona reported, for example, that the PSI Activities Assessment, or Inventory Survey:

> . . . was an essential baseline for our understanding of what campus program representatives perceive about RCR. It also provided core benchmark comparisons to other schools that used the instrument. The information we gained was at the college/broad field level, but nonetheless highlighted several potential areas for intervention:
>
> - Develop a strategy for Humanities and Arts (did they ignore the survey because they saw it as not relevant to their field?).

- Provide resources for RCR interpretation/explanation in Health Sciences.
- Provide resources for RCR activities/classes in Engineering and Sciences.
- Work across campus to add RCR statement/info on all departmental/program websites.
- Provide resources to increase "difficult discussions" in Science and Engineering.
- Create programs for postdocs and techs (orientation & in service).
- Originate ways to engage faculty in RCR programs (beyond online training).

Beyond Surveys to Assess Needs

While PSI institutions found the activities and climate surveys essential for assessing needs, they also emphasized the importance of moving beyond surveys to develop a richer understanding of how graduate schools could be most helpful to programs and their students. Columbia University, for example, reported that when the survey questions were met, by some, with confusion, the Graduate School offered to meet with the Director of Graduate Studies (DGS) and the Academic Department Administrator (ADA) to discuss questions. "These conversations," they report,

> resulted in some of the richest, most revealing information about the departments' climate and culture for RCR/PSI training. Similarly, when we first started our project, we met, department by department, with graduate students and post-doctoral fellows in an open forum discussion over lunch. We asked one question: "About which RCR/PSI topics do you wish you could have more conversations in the department?" The resulting discussion never lasted less than hour as the students and post-docs talked about the department culture and their need for information. They made it clear they wanted these conversations to occur with their advisors/PIs. And they were equally adamant that the mentors should know to initiate these conversations to provide the information students wanted rather than waiting for students to ask.

Columbia University added that it was important to involve skilled facilitators in these discussions:

> Once we learned how useful it was to conduct additional needs assessment through face-to-face meetings and conversation, it helped to have someone who could guide groups of students and post-docs, as well as DGSs and ADAs, in conversations without fear of "airing the department's dirty laundry," of the information being repeated or reported in inappropriate ways, or of consequences and retribution.

In sum, creating buy-in into the needs assessment process requires good communication, skilled facilitators with good listening skills, good will, the assurance of good and meaningful data, and a good plan for follow up so results can be translated into better programs. Coordination across multiple campus units may be necessary to implement a well-designed communication strategy. However, graduate schools are uniquely qualified to make sure that all of the various considerations required for an effective communication strategy are taken into account in shaping an effective needs assessment strategy.

PART III

Approaches to Assessing RCR and Scholarly Integrity Programs

Chapter 9.
Assessing Institutional Activities and Resources with Baseline Findings

The approach to assessment taken by PSI institutions included a variety of activities such as surveys, focus groups and face to face meetings, pre- and post-tests, and satisfaction questionnaires. As described earlier in this book, two instruments developed out of the project or through collaboration with participating PSI graduate schools were adopted in common by all participants across the project: the *Research Integrity Inventory Survey*, developed by CGS, and the *Survey of Organizational Research Climate* (Martinson and Thrush, 2008; Thrush et al., 2011). This chapter and Chapter 10 describe the baseline, aggregate data from these two surveys and discuss some possible ways in which universities might use these data and the associated survey instruments for benchmarking purposes or for internal formative assessment purposes as they seek to develop and enhance scholarly integrity programs.

A Common Assessment Strategy

As noted in Part I, a key component of the PSI approach that distinguished it from prior CGS multi-university initiatives in RCR was a common assessment strategy shared by all awardees. The strategy was designed to enable participants to identify institutional needs, promote cross-campus dialogue about possible solutions, and compare approaches to meeting those needs with other institutions. The intention behind the development of a common assessment strategy was to provide graduate schools with tools and data that would be useful, for example, to identify curricular gaps in specific graduate programs and colleges or to potentially remedy differences in perception between faculty and students about the quality of RCR training. In the future, this approach may also facilitate evidence-based discussion about which of the promising practices adopted through this project proved to be most effective enhancing research and scholarly integrity.

The PSI assessment strategy builds on some of the results of prior CGS RCR initiatives. *Best Practices in Graduate Education for RCR* (Council of Graduate Schools, 2009) concluded by recommending a three-tiered approach to assessment:

1. An assessment of the institutional climate for research integrity;
2. An "inventory of institutional practices in RCR education"; and
3. Student "learning and retention" of the knowledge and principles acquired.

The PSI approach to assessment moved forward on the first two recommendations using the two data collection instruments noted above: the *Research Integrity Inventory Survey* and the *Survey of Organizational Research Climate*. Although PSI awardees expressed a willingness to field-test a third data collection instrument to assess graduate student learning and retention of RCR knowledge, the planning committee advised that this should not be required in the request for proposals unless an instrument could be identified in advance that would be ready in time for implementation. While project participants expressed a willingness to adopt and test one instrument that was still in the development stage, that instrument was not yet available for PSI use, and limitations of other existing instruments to assess the range of learning objectives discouraged their adoption in this project.[16] PSI institutions used approaches that were appropriate to their programs and objectives, as identification of a single, common instrument for assessing graduate student learning in research and scholarly integrity proved to be a challenge across such a diverse range of programs and disciplines.

Research Integrity Inventory Survey

The *Research Integrity Inventory Survey* was designed to collect data regarding the scope and nature of activities and resources at the level of the graduate degree program or other campus unit in order to enhance graduate schools'

---

16. Institutions used a variety of different learning assessment tools in prior CGS RCR initiatives (including CITI program certification and module completion (https://www.citiprogram.org/default.asp), the Vanderbilt University Medical Center Test of RCR Knowledge, the Defining Issues Test (DIT), and locally developed surveys and pre- and post-tests). See CGS (2008) and Appendix F, Resources.

understanding of how these activities might complement and inform central campus RCR efforts. The inventory was conducted using a questionnaire with twelve questions and 209 question items. These questions were aimed at understanding: the *policy environment* within which graduate departments/programs function, *practices and procedures* in place to impart principles associated with scholarly integrity, and the modes of exposure through which scholarly integrity is embedded into graduate education though *curricular integration* (courses, workshops) and other modes of delivery and/or access (mentoring and advising, online resources, print resources, and independent research).

Awardee institutions were asked to administer the survey to one individual per program (typically a department chair or director of graduate studies) who was deemed most knowledgeable about scholarly integrity policies, practices, and modes of instruction and exposure to RCR content. The graduate deans who served as PIs for the PSI projects collectively decided to distribute the questionnaire to all programs or departments in online and, in at least one case, hard copy formats. Respondents were encouraged to answer all questions to the best of their ability on behalf of the graduate institution, department, and/or program. Although the survey generated 261 total responses, rigorous cleaning and editing generated 240 usable responses.[17] None of the data were weighted or subjected to any other treatment.

For the purposes of this analysis, data from all institutions were aggregated. Pennsylvania State University generated more responses (75) than any other participating institution. Forty-four respondents were from the University of Arizona, 39 were from the University of Alabama at Birmingham, 37 were from Emory University, 29 were from Columbia University, and 16 were from Michigan State University.

Policy Environment

The *Research Integrity Inventory Survey* included five questions aimed at informing the extent to which policies and institutional norms were in place to support scholarly integrity. Specifically, respondents were asked to indicate whether or not:

---

17. CGS project staff used the data cleaning process recommended by Van den Broeck, Argeseanu, Eeckels, and Herbst (2005)

- They had a departmental committee with responsibility for facilitating the education of all departmental personnel on responsible conduct of research and scholarly activities;
- Training in research and scholarly integrity was required for graduate students, faculty, postdoctoral fellows, and technical staff;
- The department/program helped interpret ethical conduct policies and their implementation;
- Their department/program reviewed ethical policies and their implementation; and
- Communication of RCR and research ethics topics to trainees (i.e., postdoctoral fellows, graduate students, undergraduate students, technical staff, etc.) was considered in tenure and promotion processes.

Generally speaking, the majority of respondents perceive that formal policies and procedures that might otherwise support the communication and integration of scholarly integrity are non-existent, and in some instances, not necessary (see Figure 1). For instance, 74% of respondents reported that a departmental committee with responsibility for facilitating the education of all departmental personnel on responsible conduct of research and scholarly activities either did not exist or was in planning phases. Some stated that such policies are not necessary because faculty already have a "long history of ethical behavior" and are "presumed" to be responsible. Similarly, 62% of respondents stated that ethical policies were not reviewed or were in planning phases, and 64% reported that the communication of responsible research practices to trainees (such as graduate students) was not considered in the tenure process. (To view findings by selected broad fields, subfields, and disciplines, please refer to the PSI Dashboard at: http://cgsnet.org /benchmarking/best-practices-data/PSI-dashboard).

Figure 1.
Summary of Policy-Related Findings

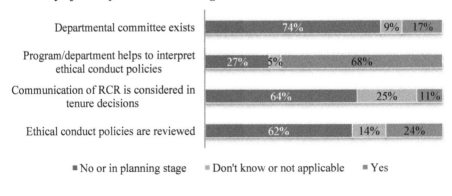

A number of respondents offered specific opinions about the need and relevance of such explicit policies and practices, a few of which are below:

> We have never had significant problems in this area at the graduate student or faculty levels. There is an implied honor code in our community that appears to function very effectively. I am not sure we need to be too much more explicit about research misconduct.

> Responsible research is always, implicitly, and fundamentally a part of . . . discourse, teaching, and research. It would only need to be considered in the breach.

> This is considered part of the expectations of the job description as much as holding class, meeting with students during office hours, or attending faculty meetings. It is not exceeding an expectation which would be rewarded in our merit driven system.

Such statements can help to clarify differences among different groups and individuals in what is meant by research integrity and responsible conduct of research, where and why enhancements may be needed, and areas in which policies and practices, and central and program-level activities, may be designed to complement and reinforce one another.

Practices and Procedures

The *Research Integrity Inventory Survey* used five questions to gauge the extent to which *practices and procedures* were in place to impart principles associated with scholarly integrity, including whether or not:

- The department/program promoted "difficult discussions" regarding research and scholarly integrity through courses, workshops, and/or seminars;
- The department/program holds forums to address the responsible conduct of research and scholarly activities;
- Information about responsible conduct of research and scholarly practices is included on their web site;

- New graduate students, new faculty, new postdoctoral fellows, and new technical staff received information about research and scholarly integrity via an orientation; and
- The communication of responsible research practices to trainees (i.e., postdoctoral fellows, graduate students, undergraduate students, technical staff, etc.) was recognized or rewarded in assessments of faculty.

The extent to which RCR and responsible research and scholarly integrity are incorporated into practices and procedures at the six participating institutions, according to survey respondents, is mixed. As shown in Figure 2, a large majority (94%) of respondents indicated that their graduate students are exposed to research and scholarly activities information at orientation. New faculty, new postdoctoral fellows, and new research staff enjoy significantly less exposure to information regarding scholarly integrity during orientation.

Figure 2.
Exposure to RCR Topics via Orientation by Status

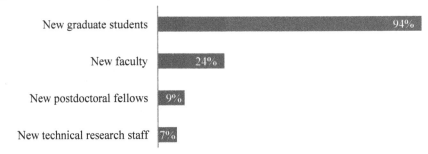

As illustrated in Figure 3, only 12% of respondents stated that the communication of responsible research practices to trainees was recognized or rewarded in faculty assessments, and only 16% stated that RCR and research and scholarly integrity information is available on the departmental/program web site. By contrast, 39% held "difficult discussions," and 52% held forums to address RCR and scholarly activities (See Appendix E for question wording and included examples of "difficult discussions.") The most frequently mentioned venue for such forums was courses, some of which appear to be dedicated entirely to responsible conduct of research, ethics, or scholarly integrity, while others appear to impart RCR and responsible research information as just one module in a full course. Seminars and workshops were also cited as common forum modes, as well as meetings, colloquia, roundtable, and guest speakers. Information on these topics is widely lacking from departmental/program web sites, according to respondents.

Figure 3.
Summary of Four Practices and Procedures-Related Findings

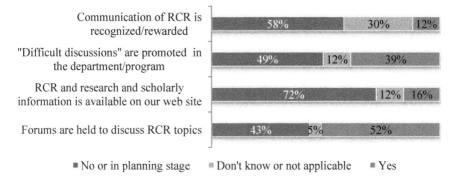

Modes of Faculty Exposure to RCR

With respect to the sources from which faculty gain understanding of scholarly integrity, their knowledge tends to depend on their own independent research of the topic, not through any formal training or workshop. For instance, nearly two-thirds (63%) of respondents[18] reported that faculty learn about the responsible conduct of research with respect to peer review via independent research. Nearly the same percentage of respondents (62%) reported that faculty learn about data acquisition, management, sharing, and ownership via independent research. Print and/or web-based materials appear to be common sources of information for faculty with respect to discipline-specific topics, such as the use of human subjects, animal subjects, and hazardous substances.

Generally speaking, respondents seemed to feel as though the onus of scholarly integrity training for faculty is on the faculty themselves. In the words of one respondent, "Individual faculty advise students, graduate and undergraduate, about standards of ethical conduct in their research. We assume the faculty are serious scholars and people of integrity. No one in [our institution] presumes to tell them how to conduct their research, although we do have IRB officers whom they sometimes consult about policies and procedures." At least one respondent, however, seemed to suggest that the presumption that faculty should already have this knowledge may be false, offering this: "The

---

18. Recall that "respondents" were typically department chairs or directors of graduate study in a program. The Inventory was not directly administered to faculty.

people who really need this training are senior level PIs and lab directors. They can teach ethics by modeling good ethical behavior. Moreover, the training that everyone needs is not at a terribly advanced level but rather nuts and bolts stuff about authorship, misconduct, deviance and noncompliance, etc."

Curricular Integration

One of the key findings from this survey points to the lack of diversity in the modes of RCR instruction (e.g., face to face, coursework, web, print, workshops/colloquia, etc.) to graduate students. When asked how graduate students currently receive instruction in each of seven general RCR topics applicable to all fields (including data acquisition and management, conflicts of interest and commitment, research misconduct, publications practices and responsible authorship, mentor and trainee responsibilities, and collaborative research), between 74% and 80% of respondents reported that all areas were covered in the advising and mentoring relationship. Less than 60% and as few as 35% reported that information about these topics were embedded in courses or classroom instruction. Less than 40%, and, in most cases less than one-third of respondents reported that students received exposure to these topics in workshops, print materials, or web-based instruction.

While it is perhaps reassuring that most chairs and directors of graduate study expect that instruction in such topics is already covered in advising and mentoring, the expectations that this is so are often implicit rather than explicit. Some respondents were skeptical that such transference of information happens at all. In the words of one respondent, "We're developing these resources for postdocs. Frankly I wouldn't guarantee that they get it from their advisors." In the words of another, "Obviously, trainees can learn from mentors, IF the mentors are proactive and teach on these issues; but of course not all do."

Possible Uses for *Research Integrity Inventory Survey* Findings

The *Research Integrity Inventory Survey* provided participating institutions with key information about the extent to which educational resources and activities already existed in their graduate programs, in large part, before the Project for Scholarly Integrity interventions were put into place. The results assisted graduate schools and project leaders in identifying areas in which there may be unmet needs or where there may already be strong existing resources to which they might refer others. Results may also be useful for identifying where lingering misperceptions about why RCR education is important, for example, that it entails nothing more than knowing a simple set of rules or is merely a matter of personal integrity or "honor," as some open ended responses suggested. Such perceptions may result in resistance to recognizing or meeting real instructional needs or a lack of support for student participation in relevant opportunities.

Results may also serve to identify situations in which faculty with oversight responsibilities for the quality of graduate student education may share the values of the PSI (i.e., that research integrity and RCR topics *should be* addressed in the advising and mentoring relationship) but may lack the means to assess whether and to what extent expectations for mentoring and advising are being met consistently and by all. Demonstrating that data such as these collected within the PSI can be used to assist programs in developing educational resources and activities that are relevant to their students and that helps them to achieve other goals (such as successful attainment of federal funding) can help to broaden faculty support for ongoing assessment.

Chapter 10.
Assessing Organizational Research Climate with Baseline Findings from the PSI

Survey of Organizational Research Climate

The second key component of the PSI was the *Survey of Organizational Research Climate*, which was intended to assess the organizational environment for responsible research practices at the six participating institutions from the perspective of students, faculty, and other personnel. The genesis of this survey was a pre-validated version of an instrument first developed by Thrush, Vander Putten, Rapp, Pearson, Berry, and O'Sullivan (2007) and implemented in 2009 at a three-member consortium including Michigan State University, Pennsylvania State University, and the University of Wisconsin-Madison.

The centerpiece of the questionnaire was 63 climate items, posed as questions such as, "How available are advisors/supervisors to their advisees/supervisees?" Respondents were asked to rate each climate item using a five-point scale: (1) not at all; (2) somewhat; (3) moderately; (4) very; or (5) completely. Respondents who felt that they had no basis for judging were given a sixth option for this purpose. Some climate items were aimed at gauging the climate for responsible research at the institution-level, while other described the research climate at the department/program-level, hereafter referred to as the "subunit" level. Fourteen demographic/classification items were also included with the climate survey.

Using data collected by the *Survey of Organizational Research Climate* in a separate project funded by the National Institutes of Health (R21-RR025279), Martinson and Thrush (2008) performed exploratory and confirmatory factor analyses, which are analytical approaches typically used to reduce large quantities of psychometric data into a smaller number of variables, and to evaluate their variability (DeVellis, 1991). As reported in the survey user's manual, Thrush et al. (2011, and manuscript under review, February, 2012) empirically determined that 32 of the climate items were sufficient to analyze the research climate along four framing items and seven subscales. The framing items assess respondents' global perceptions of the institutional and subunit research integrity climates while the subscales below address specific aspects of the institutional and subunit climate for research integrity:

1. *Institutional RCR Resources* depicts the degree to which respondents feel as though there is adequate institutional support for RCR.
2. *Institutional Regulatory Quality* describes the adequacy of policy and regulatory supports.
3. *Subunit Integrity Norms* describes the extent to which departmental/ programmatic (i.e., subunit) norms and institutions shape RCR practices.
4. *Subunit Integrity Socialization* depicts the extent to which RCR is socialized within subunits.
5. *Subunit Advisor Advisee Relations* depicts the relationships between advisors/supervisors and their subordinates.
6. *Subunit Integrity Inhibitors* explains the extent to which certain conditions produce negative effects.
7. *Subunit Expectations* depicts fairness with respect to publishing and funding expectations.

In 2009, CGS adopted use of the pre-validated version of the *Survey of Organizational Research Climate* across all PSI awardees institutions and subsequently utilized the final 32 validated items for the analyses reported here.

The survey was administered to a broad spectrum of groups that comprise each institution's research enterprise, including graduate students, faculty, research staff, postdoctoral fellows, and others. Data from this effort were analyzed and reported according to these seven validated subscales, using the recommendations proposed by Thrush et al. (2011). For instance, individuals who either did not respond to a question item or responded using the "No Basis for Judging" category were excluded from the analyses. The survey generated 21,313 responses, 14,947 of which were used for this analysis, after excluding undergraduate students, graduate students in course-based master's programs, technicians, and research scientists. Respondents included those who performed research and were either graduate students in research master's or doctoral programs, postdoctoral trainees, or faculty. Of these, 68% earned their first bachelor's degree in the United States, and 32% earned their first bachelor's degree outside of the U.S. More than half (57%) of respondents were graduate students and roughly one-third (36%) were faculty. The remaining 7% were postdoctoral fellows. When asked to describe themselves by their discipline of their highest degree (see Figure 4), biomedical/life/health sciences represented the largest percentage of respondents by broad field (24%), followed by social sciences (18%), engineering (15%) and physical or mathematical sciences (15%).

Figure 4.
Distribution of Respondents by Discipline of Highest Degree

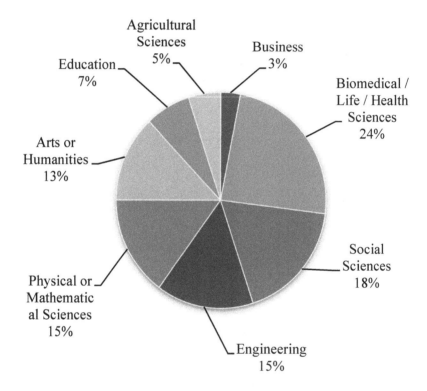

Although the data are too voluminous to summarize in this report, some highlights are worth noting. Overall differences between the perceptions of faculty and graduate students are minimal, and the proportion of positive responses are high (over 75%) for several subscale measures (e.g., with respect to program climate, university climate, and expected standards for the integrity of their scholarship). Baseline findings of the *Survey of Organizational Research Climate* are analyzed here according to recommended methodology. The sections below, and Figures 5 through 12, provide analyses of data according to the framing items and each of the seven subscales.

Framing Items

The *Framing Items* include four globally worded climate items, which describe the extent to which the institution and subunits are committed to maintaining standards of integrity in research and the degree to which the overall climate of integrity in the institution and subunits reflects high values of RCR.

As shown in Figure 5, all four of the global climate items received high ratings. No fewer than 82% of respondents, regardless of their status within their institution (i.e., faculty, postdoctoral fellows, or graduate students), rated any one of these four items as being "very" or "completely" consistent and committed.

Figure 5.
Framing Items by Status[19]

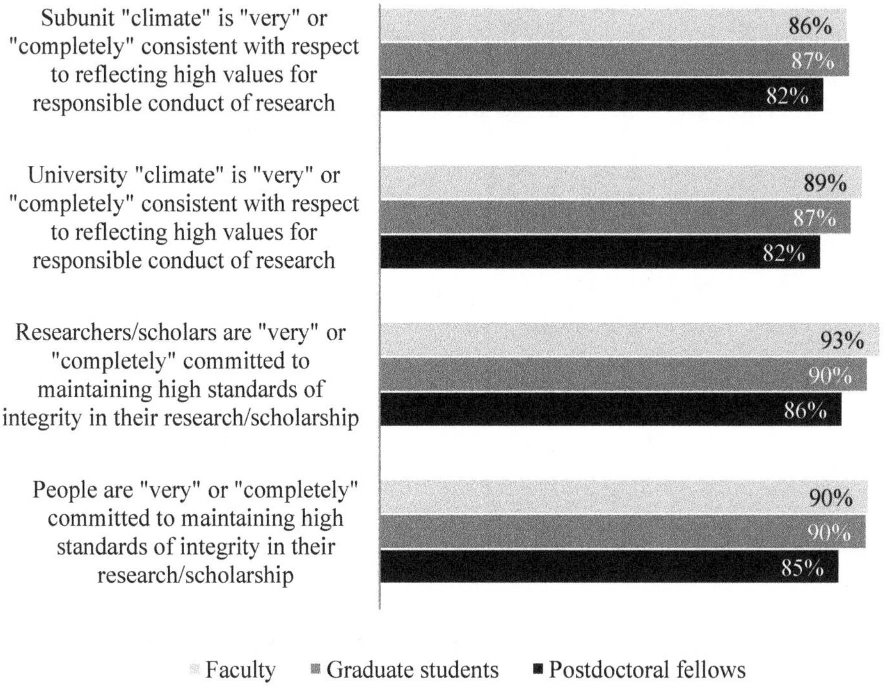

Subunit "climate" is "very" or "completely" consistent with respect to reflecting high values for responsible conduct of research — 86%, 87%, 82%

University "climate" is "very" or "completely" consistent with respect to reflecting high values for responsible conduct of research — 89%, 87%, 82%

Researchers/scholars are "very" or "completely" committed to maintaining high standards of integrity in their research/scholarship — 93%, 90%, 86%

People are "very" or "completely" committed to maintaining high standards of integrity in their research/scholarship — 90%, 90%, 85%

Faculty   Graduate students   Postdoctoral fellows

---

19. Exact question wording, developed by Thrush, et al., (2011), can be found at https://sites. google.com/site/surveyoforgresearchclimate/

Institutional RCR Resources

The collective results from six climate items convey the degree to which respondents feel as though there are adequate institutional supports for RCR and responsible research, referred to hereafter as the *Institutional RCR Resources* subscale. Seven out of ten graduate student respondents to the *Survey of Organizational Research Climate* reported that administrators were "very" or "completely" committed to supporting responsible research/scholarship, and able to communicate high expectations. Fewer graduate students (six out of ten) reported that RCR education is "very" or "completely" effective. And less than half of the graduate student respondents reported that experts are accessible when advice is needed.

Postdoctoral fellows in particular seem to feel as though institutional supports are only somewhat adequate. While faculty perceptions generally agreed with those of graduate students and postdocs and were slightly more positive on most items, they perceived an even greater need for more effective teaching in RCR. These and other findings appear in Figure 6.

Figure 6.
Institutional RCR Resources by Status[20]

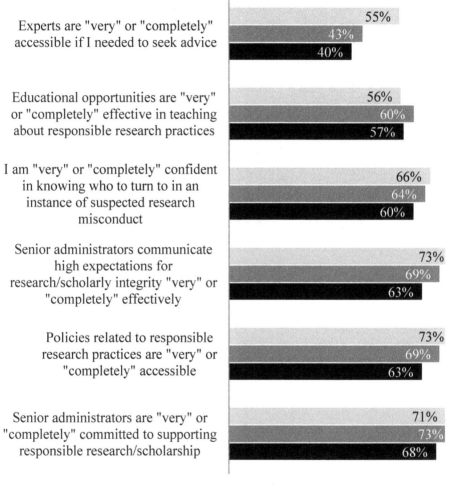

---

20. See note 19.

Institutional Regulatory Quality

The *Institutional Regulatory Quality* subscale is comprised of findings generated by three items to describe the adequacy of policy and regulatory supports. Overall, three-quarters of respondents (76%) felt that regulatory committees that review research were either "very" or "completely" respectful of researchers. Two-thirds (67%) of respondents felt that regulatory committees that review research were "very" or "completely" fair to researchers, and half (52%) reported that these boards understand the kind of research they do either "very" or "completely" well.

There were differences, however, among groups of respondents (shown in Figure 7). Faculty tended to give their institution lower ratings than post-doctoral fellows and especially graduate students. Differences were not large, but they were consistent across all three items. For instance, and as shown in Figure 7, while 55% of both graduate students and postdoctoral fellows felt that regulatory committees review research either "very" or "completely" well, 47% of faculty held the same opinion.

Figure 7.
Institutional Regulatory Quality by Status[21]

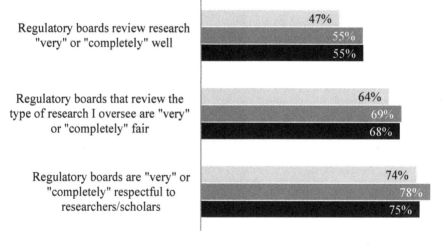

Regulatory boards review research "very" or "completely" well
- 47%
- 55%
- 55%

Regulatory boards that review the type of research I oversee are "very" or "completely" fair
- 64%
- 69%
- 68%

Regulatory boards are "very" or "completely" respectful to researchers/scholars
- 74%
- 78%
- 75%

Faculty ■ Graduate students ■ Postdoctoral fellows

---

21. See note 19.

Subunit Integrity Norms

The subscale referred to as *Subunit Integrity Norms* describes the extent to which departmental/programmatic (i.e., subunit) norms shape RCR practices. This subscale received some of the most consistently high ratings of the seven subscales, particularly among faculty and postdoctoral fellows who rated no less than 83% on any one of the four subunit integrity norms items. The percent of faculty and graduate students felt that people are "very" or "completely" committed, honest, and consistent with respect to maintaining standards of responsible research and scholarly integrity was nearly 90% in most categories.

Figure 8.
Subunit Integrity Norms by Status[22]

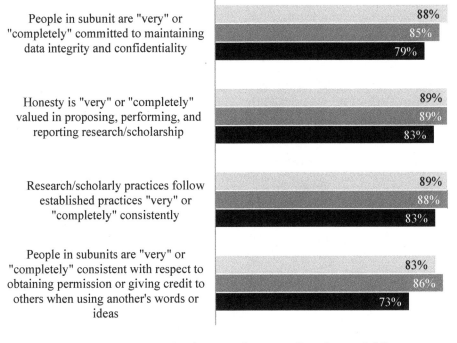

22. See note 19.

Subunit Integrity Socialization

The *Subunit Integrity Socialization* subscale used data generated by four items to depict the extent to which RCR is socialized within subunits. In contrast to the *Subunit Integrity Norms* subscale, which received some of the highest ratings of the seven subscales, the *Subunit Integrity Socialization* scale received some of the lowest ratings. Postdoctoral fellows felt that socialization was performed "very" or "completely" well between 49% and 58% of the time. Faculty felt that socialization was performed "very" or "completely" well between 55% and 65% of the time. Graduate students felt that socialization was performed "very" or "completely" well 59% to 65% of the time.

Figure 9.
Subunit Integrity Socialization by Status[23]

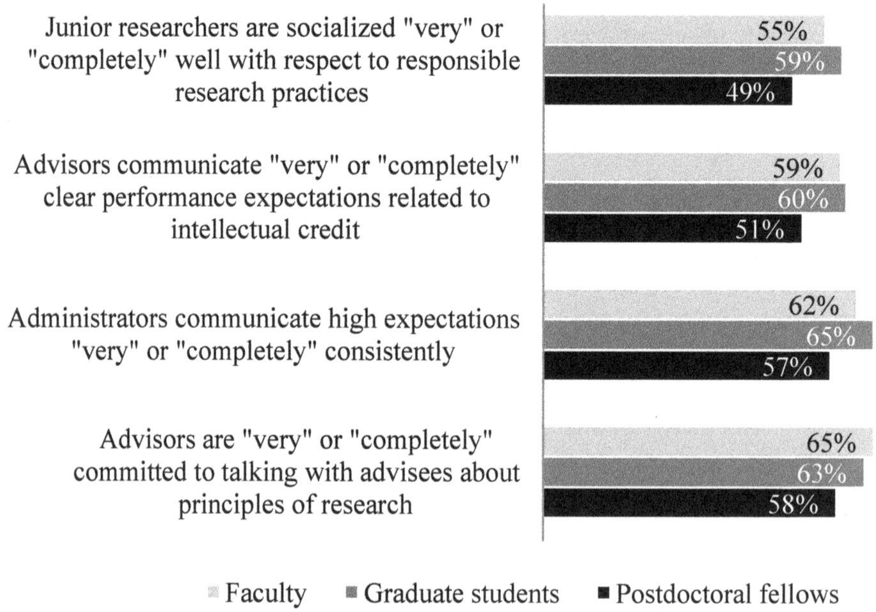

Junior researchers are socialized "very" or "completely" well with respect to responsible research practices
- 55%
- 59%
- 49%

Advisors communicate "very" or "completely" clear performance expectations related to intellectual credit
- 59%
- 60%
- 51%

Administrators communicate high expectations "very" or "completely" consistently
- 62%
- 65%
- 57%

Advisors are "very" or "completely" committed to talking with advisees about principles of research
- 65%
- 63%
- 58%

Faculty   Graduate students   Postdoctoral fellows

---

23. See note 19.

Subunit Advisor/Advisee Relations

The subscale referred to as *Subunit Advisor/Advisee Relations* describes the relationships between advisors/supervisors and their subordinates using three climate items. Specifically, it refers to the degree to which advisors treat advisees with fairness and respect, and the degree to which advisors are available to advisees and subordinates. Generally speaking, faculty, graduate students, and postdoctoral students appear to feel as though the relationships between advisors and advisees are good ones. Faculty, however, appear to feel better about these relationships than graduate students and postdoctoral fellows. Nearly four out of five faculty (79%) feel that advisors treat advisees "very" or "completely" fairly, compared to 71% of graduate students and 65% of postdoctoral fellows.

Figure 10.
Subunit Advisor/Advisee Relations by Status[24]

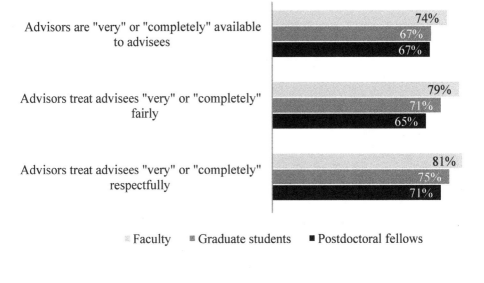

Advisors are "very" or "completely" available to advisees — 74%, 67%, 67%

Advisors treat advisees "very" or "completely" fairly — 79%, 71%, 65%

Advisors treat advisees "very" or "completely" respectfully — 81%, 75%, 71%

Faculty   Graduate students   Postdoctoral fellows

---

24. See note 19.

Subunit Integrity Inhibitors

The *Subunit Integrity Inhibitors* subscale used six items to explain the extent to which certain conditions produce negative effects within subunits (i.e., departments, programs). Because this scale was reverse coded to match the other subscales, it is arguably more difficult to interpret, yet it reveals some of the most interesting differences between faculty, graduate students, and postdoctoral fellows. Neither faculty, nor graduate students, nor postdoctoral fellows reported significant difficulties due to inadequate human or material resources. Generally speaking, faculty feel that people are not guarded in their communications with one another, competitive, pressured to secure external funding, or pressured to publish. Graduate students and postdoctoral students, on the other hand, are more likely than faculty to feel as though people are guarded in communicating with one another, that their peers are competitive, and that there is pressure to publish and secure external funding. These findings appear in Figure 11.

Figure 11.
Subunit Integrity Inhibitors by Status[25]

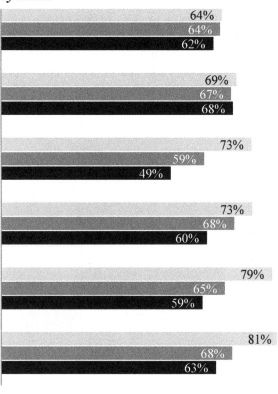

Insufficient human resources is not a hindrance to research	64% / 64% / 62%
Insufficient equipment, space, and technology is not a hindrance to research	69% / 67% / 68%
People are not at all or only somewhat guarded in their communications with one another	73% / 59% / 49%
People are not competitive	73% / 68% / 60%
There is little pressure to secure external funding	79% / 65% / 59%
There is little pressure to publish	81% / 68% / 63%

Faculty   Graduate students   Postdoctoral fellows

---

25. See note 19.

Subunit Expectations

Finally, the *Subunit Expectations* subscale depicts the extent to which respondents feel that expectations with respect to publishing and funding are fair. Two items are used in this subscale, and both received generally high ratings regardless of respondent status (see Figure 12). For instance, three-quarters of all respondents felt that publishing expectations were "very" or "completely" fair. Between 64% and 67% of respondents felt that expectations with respect to obtaining external funding were "very" or "completely" fair.

Figure 12.
Subunit Expectations by Status[26]

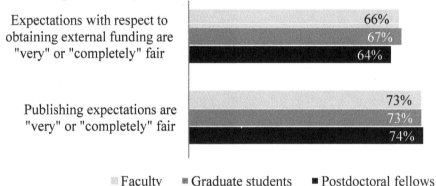

Expectations with respect to obtaining external funding are "very" or "completely" fair — 66%, 67%, 64%

Publishing expectations are "very" or "completely" fair — 73%, 73%, 74%

Faculty ■ Graduate students ■ Postdoctoral fellows

Climate Survey Summary

As discussed above, data generated by the *Survey of Organizational Research Climate* were evaluated using seven subscales that constitute 32 climate items. In some instances, faculty, graduate students, and postdoctoral fellows share a common view of the organizational climate. For example, percentages of graduate students, faculty, and postdoctoral fellows who rated each of the two survey questions related to *Subunit Expectations* as either "very" or "completely" varied by no more than two percentage points. This suggests that there is relative harmony among respondents with respect to the expectations. In other cases, faculty, graduate students, and postdoctoral fellows do not share a common view.

---

26. See note 19.

With few exceptions, faculty generally rated climate items higher than graduate students who, in turn, rated climate items higher than postdoctoral fellows. Two of the subscales, *Subunit Socialization* and *Institutional Regulatory Quality,* reflected a different pattern wherein students rated climate items higher than faculty. Both of these subscales generated relatively low overall means, suggesting that they may be areas in need of evaluation and improvement.

A different way to portray the results of the *Survey of Organizational Research Climate* is in aggregate. Means of all survey questions, with responses ranging from "not at all," which has a value of 1, to "completely," which has a value of 5, were calculated to provide a single depiction of all data generated by the survey. Respondents indicating that they had no basis for judging were excluded. For example, all responses to all three survey questions that constitute the *Institutional Regulatory Quality* subscale were used to calculated an overall mean of 3.72 (see Figure 13 below).

Figure 13.
Summary of Composites

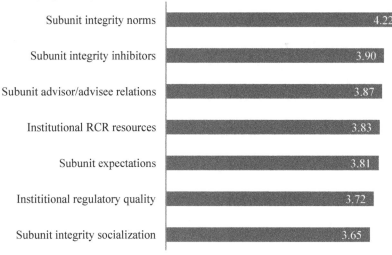

As shown in Figure 13, the overall means ranged from 3.65 to 4.22 across the seven subscales. The subscale with the highest overall mean was *Subunit Integrity Norms* (4.22) followed by *Subunit Integrity Inhibitors* (3.90), and *Advisor/Advisee Relations* (3.87). The relatively high overall mean for *Subunit Integrity Norms* suggests that, among survey respondents, the norms embodied in departments/programs that are aimed at supporting research and scholarly integrity appear to be particularly strong and consistent.

Future Data Dissemination

This report highlights only a fraction of the data generated by the *Research Integrity Inventory Survey* and *Survey of Organizational Climate*. Additional analysis can be performed at various broad field, subfield, and discipline levels, as well as by certain attributes, so long as the data are not so small that they may inadvertently disclose any particular institution or program. One safeguard against accidental disclosure was the establishment of a minimum threshold: data would only be reported in instances where five or more institutions were represented at the broad field, subfield, or discipline level. The broad fields, six reportable subfields, and eight reportable disciplines appear in Appendix D. Moreover, CGS has developed an online dashboard, viewable at: www.cgsnet.org/benchmarking/best-practices-data/PSI-dashboard. The Dashboard allows users to generate their own data summaries based upon their choice of certain variables.

Conclusion

Several awardees reported that these instruments have provided them with the most comprehensive data on RCR and research integrity activities ever collected by their institutions, and that these data are helping them prepare for new requirements for graduate RCR training by federal funders. For instance, Michigan State University's graduate dean, Karen Klomparens, and conflict of interest information officer, Terry May, presented on the development of the *Survey of Organizational Research Climate* and on its use at CGS' 2010 Summer Workshop (Klomparens & May, 2010). Additionally, the final, validated *Survey of Organizational Research Climate* was released by its developers Thrush, Martinson, Crain, and Wells (2011) for public use and has been made available under a Creative Commons license.

All of this is evidence to support the fact that, in addition to serving the broader goals of the project, PSI awardees and affiliates have made important strides in addressing many of the assessment needs identified by the National Academies report on *Integrity in Scientific Research* (2002), including:

- Lack of established measures for assessing integrity in the research environment;
- Lack of evidence to definitively support any one way to approach the problem of promoting and evaluating research integrity; and

- Need for institutional self-assessment, which is one promising approach to assessing and continually improving integrity in research. (National Research Council of the National Academies, 2002, p. 3, as cited in CGS, 2009)

While assessment is by no means the central activity of the PSI, the administration of the two surveys described above, analysis of survey data, and subsequent conversations between the graduate school and colleges and departments are providing participating universities with techniques for achieving progress on internal and collective objectives.

The instruments used by PSI participants and analyzed here are accessible through the Project for Scholarly Integrity Website (www.scholarlyintegrity.org). PSI project staff are happy to assist institutions which are curious to explore using these tools to assess institutional needs and enhance educational programs in research and scholarly integrity for graduate students.

PART IV

Tools in the
PSI Toolbox

Chapter 11.
Online Tools in
the PSI Toolbox

he Project for Scholarly Integrity resulted in a variety of "tools" designed
for use by graduate schools to develop and enhance graduate education
in research and scholarly integrity. CGS promoted and made publicly
available the assessment tools described earlier in this publication through a
variety of CGS events and publications, and presentations and publications by
PSI graduate deans and CGS project staff highlighted how PSI participants used
those assessment tools to enhance their PSI programs. CGS also developed
two interactive online tools: a dedicated PSI website (www.scholarlyintegrity.
org) that documented project achievements in an ongoing way throughout the
duration of the PSI and served as a clearinghouse of resources and information
relevant to the enhancement of graduate education in research and scholarly
integrity, and the PSI Dashboard (http://www.cgsnet.org/benchmarking/best-
practices-data/PSI-dashboard), which provides visitors with interactive access
to a wealth of project data. We conclude with a brief description of each of
these online tools, and encourage readers to make use of these resources.

PSI Website

The PSI Website, launched in January 2009, was designed to serve as a
resource for project participants and for all others seeking to better institutionalize RCR education for graduate students on their campuses. The primary
goal for the site was to give users quick, easy access to materials developed
by awardees and information about their projects as well as to serve as a gate-
way to other quality resources. The website and the information architecture
were developed with non-specialists foremost in mind (such as senior administrators, project directors, faculty, and students). The PSI Website served as
a clearinghouse of resources related to scholarly integrity and RCR and provided an electronic forum in which awardees, affiliates institutions, and others

could exchange information and advice about building institution-wide efforts to institutionalize research ethics education. This website includes an overview of the Project for Scholarly Integrity, links to documents and tools developed for the project, information about each institution and a wide variety of general and institutional resources, tools, curricula, etc. The website contains a wealth of invaluable information for graduate deans and others seeking to develop and enhance scholarly integrity and RCR education. This website may be accessed directly (at www.scholarlyintegrity.org) or through the CGS Website (http://www.cgsnet.org/scholarly-integrity-and-responsible-conduct-research-rcr).

Through the PSI website, visitors may access a wide variety of useful collections and resources:

The PSI Online Resource Library

A key feature of the PSI Website is a searchable database of resources on scholarly integrity and RCR. This online resource library was developed for all members of the graduate community, including deans and administrators working to implement new, institution-wide structures of training and oversight; faculty members involved in ethics education and training in the Responsible Conduct of Research; and researchers (including graduate students) working to understand specific topics in scholarly integrity and research ethics. There is also a wide range of topics represented in the online library: some resources discuss problems of general interest to the scientific community, while others are discipline-specific. The resource library includes over 760 resources and is searchable by 69 categories. The navigation menu allows visitors to easily search by keyword and/or by 16 RCR topics, as well as by other categories in areas such as: approaches to institutional change, assessment, sample curricula (case studies, course syllabi, online modules, etc.), policies and codes, and international issues.

Interactive Blog

The PSI Website hosts an interactive "blog" that allows PSI participants and others to communicate with each other and the broader graduate community on various topics in research ethics education. Blog entries typical consist of short, conversational pieces intended to raise awareness about an issue or spark discussion about selected topics. The blog includes thought provoking entries on topics such as: the use of video vignettes in RCR training, with active links to video resources; common challenges surrounding institution-wide RCR Training and possible approaches to overcoming these challenges; the responsibilities of institutions and funders to address predatory behavior in the scientific community.

The blog also includes a "blogroll," or set of links to other carefully-vetted blog sites, where visitors may gather additional insight into hot topics and current issues in research and scholarly integrity.[27]

---

27. External sites on the blogroll at the time of publication of this manuscript included: American Journal of Bioethics; the Research Ethics Blog; Women's Bioethics Project; the Institutional Review Blog; Nature Publishing Group; the Scientific Misconduct Blog; Health Care Renewal; Medical Writing, Editing, and Grantsmanship; Peer-to-Peer; Adventures in Ethics and Science; Alliance for Human Research Protection; and Science Progress.

The PSI Newsletter

Since November, 2008, PSI project staff have compiled and issued a "PSI Newsletter" to inform PSI partners and the broader graduate community about activities specific to the PSI, activities on PSI partner campuses, and other resources and events relevant to research and scholarly integrity. Subscription is free and subscribers represent a large number of U.S. institutions. All PSI newsletters are archived on the PSI website.

University Press Releases

Four PSI awardees (Emory, MSU, PSU, and the University of Wisconsin-Madison) and three Affiliates (Purdue, University of West Florida, and Wake Forest University) provided links to press releases on their participation in the PSI.

Other Relevant PSI Materials and Resources

The website also archives the original framework paper that accompanied the Request for Proposals, the RFP, contact information for PSI participant leaders, and links to PowerPoint presentations and published materials by PSI PI's and co-PI's about individual PSI projects and by CGS project staff about the PSI.

PSI Dashboard

Both surveys used to collect data in support of the Project for Scholarly Integrity (PSI) generated large quantities of data. The *Research Integrity Inventory Survey* generated 240 responses, and the *Survey of Organizational Research Climate* generated over 21,000 responses. Although the data were reported in aggregate in Chapters 9 and 10 of this monograph, CGS saw an opportunity to create the PSI Dashboard, an online component allowing users to interact with the data themselves. The data may be filtered according to any one of 15 fields/disciplines, which represents instances in which five or more institutions were represented by the survey responses. This five-institution threshold was established in order to protect the confidentiality of respondents. Users may also e-mail and print results generated by the PSI Dashboard in pdf format. This online component resides on the CGS web site at www.cgsnet. org/benchmarking/best-practices-data/PSI-dashboard.

Research Integrity Inventory

Data from 11 of the 12 questions in the *Research Integrity Inventory Survey* are available on the PSI Dashboard. Only one question was not included due to its open-ended nature. The data were sorted into three categories: policies, practices, and modes of exposure. Within each category, as shown in the image below, users may select from specific questions as well as any one of 15 fields/disciplines. Users may also review aggregate data as well by selecting "All Fields."

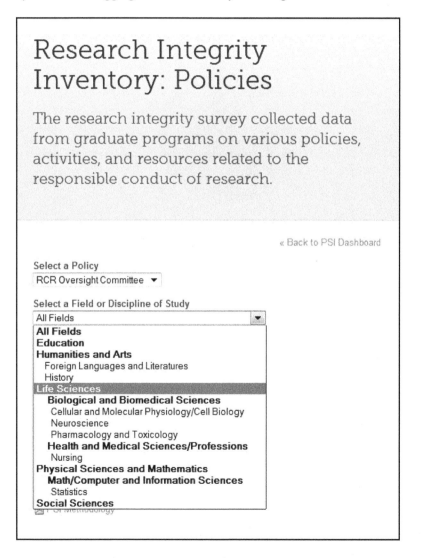

Data from the *Research Integrity Inventory Survey* are portrayed in either a pie-chart (as shown below), or a table, depending upon the nature of the survey question. In either case, the results are presented in percentages. In the case of the pie-charts, the number of responses are also presented.

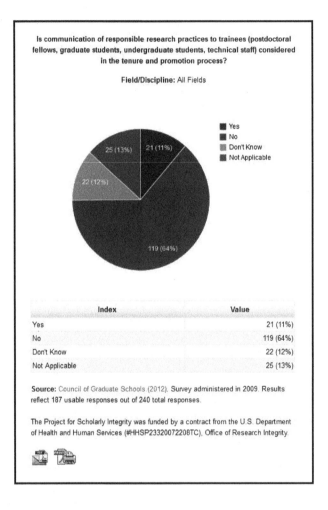

Climate Survey

Data from 29 of the 63 climate items listed in the *Survey of Organizational Research Climate* are available on the PSI Dashboard. For purposes of the PSI Dashboard, these 29 were sorted into five categories: leadership, policies, practices and resources, know-how, and climate. As illustrated below, results are displayed using bar charts, and specific counts and percentages appear when users "hover" over the bar of interest.

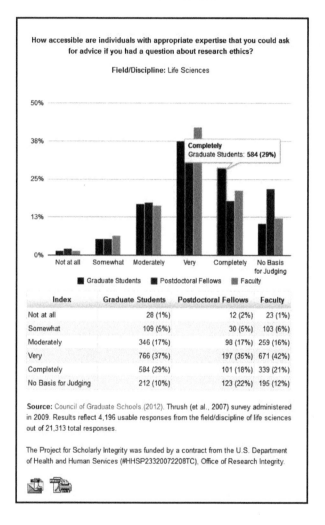

How accessible are individuals with appropriate expertise that you could ask for advice if you had a question about research ethics?

Field/Discipline: Life Sciences

Completely
Graduate Students: 584 (29%)

Index	Graduate Students	Postdoctoral Fellows	Faculty
Not at all	28 (1%)	12 (2%)	23 (1%)
Somewhat	109 (5%)	30 (5%)	103 (6%)
Moderately	346 (17%)	98 (17%)	259 (16%)
Very	766 (37%)	197 (35%)	671 (42%)
Completely	584 (29%)	101 (18%)	339 (21%)
No Basis for Judging	212 (10%)	123 (22%)	195 (12%)

Source: Council of Graduate Schools (2012). Thrush (et al., 2007) survey administered in 2009. Results reflect 4,196 usable responses from the field/discipline of life sciences out of 21,313 total responses.

The Project for Scholarly Integrity was funded by a contract from the U.S. Department of Health and Human Services (#HHSP23320072208TC), Office of Research Integrity.

Although all 63 climate items and seven subscales determined by Thrush et al. (2011) were used to describe the results of the survey in this publication, only 29 climate items were used for the PSI Dashboard. This decision was made for two reasons. First, the interpretation of the results according to each of the seven subscales requires some conceptual and methodological explanation. Users of online data visualizations, such as the PSI Dashboard, typically need and expect quick, easy to interpret data formats. Second, incorporating all seven subscales would have necessitated using all 63 climate items, which, again, is too many for portrayal on the PSI Dashboard. CGS identified 29 climate items as being of most interest to graduate deans and used those for the PSI Dashboard.

Some combinations of data that are filtered by the PSI Dashboard result in a small number of eligible responses. For instance, even though the discipline of neuroscience was represented by at least five institutions, it is a small discipline. As a consequence, some of the results generated based upon filtering data affiliated with neuroscience may become magnified. Our careful attempt to footnote each figure was an attempt to describe the scope and size of the data being portrayed, and reduce the likelihood of misinterpretation.

Conclusion

The Project for Scholarly Integrity encompassed an extraordinary breadth and amount of activity, far exceeding the original goals of CGS and funded institutions. At each of the six institutions, for example, the PSI ultimately extended to include more students, faculty, researchers, and fields than originally envisioned. Each university targeted the behavioral and biomedical sciences as required to support the goals of CGS, the Office of Research Integrity, and the Department of Health and Human Services to improve the quality of preparation of graduate students in these disciplines in the responsible conduct of research. Beyond that goal, however, every participating institution believed so strongly in the value and potential benefits of the PSI approach that they all decided, during the early stages of the project, to expand their initiatives to include all disciplines. They did so with the conviction that by expanding the reach and visibility of the PSI, the impact on target disciplines would also be greater. Each university also embraced the broad vision of the project, endorsed so strongly by members of the advisory committee, that improvements in graduate education for RCR depends upon a comprehensive institutional vision for program development.

A central lesson of the project is that true institutionalization of RCR benefits most from collaboration among institutions, collective efforts to assess needs and impact using comparable techniques and measures, and central coordination. Such coordination is required to allow project leaders to come together, to facilitate the exchange of best practices, and to document the impact of those projects. Another important overarching lesson of the project is that an evidence-based approach to the development and improvement of research integrity programs is possible. The PSI proved the feasibility, under the strong leadership of graduate deans, of a collective and collaborative approach to needs assessment that is integrated into institutional efforts to improve policies and practices related to graduate education in RCR. All agreed that the next step to ensure that this work continues to gain traction nationally will be to continue to assess needs and document impact; however, the true measure of impact on learning and research conduct will require the leadership and participation of more institutions and individuals in replicating such programs nationwide.

The Council of Graduate Schools looks forward to working with the entire graduate community to highlight promising and best practices in an ongoing way and to foster the improvement of graduate education for research and scholarly integrity.

References

American Association for the Advancement of Science (AAAS) and the United States Office of Research Integrity (ORI). (2000). *The role and activities of scientific societies in promoting research integrity: A report on a conference.* Retrieved from http://www.aaas.org/

Bell, D. F. and James, D. L. (2011, March 1). Update on mandatory Responsible Conduct of Research (RCR) training in light of the *America COMPETES Act of 2007* and federal grant applications (NIH). Memorandum. Durham, North Carolina. Retrieved from http://gradschool.duke.edu/

Bush, V. (1945). *Science the endless frontier.* Washington, D.C.: United States Government Printing Office. Retrieved from http://www.nsf.gov/

Casadevall, A. and Fang, F.C. (2012, March). Reforming science: Methodological and cultural reforms. *Infection and Immunity,* 80(3), 891-896.

Committee on Freedom and Responsibility in the conduct of Science (CFRS). (2008, September). *Promoting the integrity of science and the scientific record.* Retrieved from http://www.icsu.org/publications/cfrs-statements/

Council of Graduates Schools. (2006). *Graduate education for the responsible conduct of research.* Washington, DC: Author.

Council of Graduate Schools. (2009). *Best practices in graduate education for the responsible conduct of research.* Washington, DC: Author.

Crow, M. and Bozeman, B. (1998). *Limited by Design—R&D Laboratories in the U.S. National Innovation System.* New York : Columbia University Press.

Denecke, D. (2008). *The Project for Scholarly Integrity in Graduate Education: A Framework for Collaborative Action.* Washington, DC: Council of Graduate Schools.

DeVellis, R.F. (1991). *Scale development: Theory and applications.* Newbury Park, CA: Sage Publications.

Epstein, D. (2006, April 24). The real science ethics issues. *Inside Higher Ed.* Retrieved from http://www.insidehighered.com/

Fanelli, D. (2009, May). How many scientists fabricate and falsify research? A systematic review and meta-analysis of survey data. *Plos One,* 4(5), e5738. doi:10.1371/journal.pone.0005738

Institute of Medicine. (1989). *The responsible conduct of research in the health sciences: Report of a study by a committee on the responsible conduct of research.* Washington, DC: National Academy.

Jonas, H. (1984). *The imperative of responsibility: In search of an ethics for the technological age.* Chicago, IL: University of Chicago Press.

Klomparens, K. & May, T. (2010, July). *Project on scholarly integrity.* Presented at the Council of Graduate Schools' 2010 New Deans Institute and Summer Workshop, San Juan, Puerto Rico. Retrieved from http://www.cgsnet.org/

Martinson, B.C., Anderson, M. S., & de Vries, R. (2005, June 8). Scientists behaving badly. *Nature,* 435, 737-738.

Mayer, T. and Steneck, N. (2007, November). Final report to ESF and ORI World Conference on Research Integrity: Fostering responsible research. European Science Foundation (ESF) and the U.S. Office of Research Integrity (ORI). Retrieved from http://www.esf.org/

National Research Council of the National Academies. (2002). *Integrity in scientific research: creating an environment that promotes responsible conduct.* Washington, DC: The National Academies Press.

National Science Board. (2010). Science and Engineering Indicators 2010. Arlington, VA: National Science Foundation.

National Science Foundation (NSF). (2010, March 3). Responsible conduct of research (RCR) frequently asked questions. Retrieved from http://www.nsf.gov/

National Science Foundation, Division of Science Resources Statistics. (2002, April). Science and Engineering Indicators-2002. Arlington, VA: Author.

Office of Inspector General, National Science Foundation. Semiannual report to Congress, September 2011 (http://www.nsf.gov/pubs/2012/oig12001/oig12001.pdf).

Office of Research Integrity (ORI). (2011). Definition of research misconduct. Retrieved from http://ori.hhs.gov/

Steneck, N. H. (2007). *ORI introduction to the responsible conduct of research.* Washington, DC: Department of Health and Human Services.

Thrush, C. R., Martinson, B.C., Crain, A.L., & Wells, J.A. (2011, March). *User's manual for the survey of organizational research climate.* Retrieved August 12, 2011 from https://sites.google.com/site/surveyoforgresearchclimate/

Thrush, C. R., Putten, J. V., Rapp, C. G., Pearson, L. C., Berry, K. S., & O'Sullivan, P. S. (2007). Content validation of the organizational climate for research integrity (OCRI) survey. *Journal of Empirical Research on Human Research Ethics, 2*(4), 35-52. doi:10.1525/jer.2007.2.4.35

Van den Broeck, J., Argeseanu Cunningham, S., Eeckels, R., & Herbst, K. (2005). Data cleaning: Detecting, diagnosing, and editing data abnormalities. *PLoS Medicine, 2*(10), e267. doi:10.1371/journal.pmed.0020267

Appendices

Appendix A

Project for Scholarly Integrity Awardees and Affiliates

PSI Awardee Institutions

Columbia University
Emory University
Michigan State University
The Pennsylvania State University

University of Alabama at Birmingham
University of Arizona
University of Wisconsin, Madison

PSI Affiliate Institutions

Duke University
Georgia Institute of Technology
Howard University
Marquette University
Northern Arizona University
Princeton University
Purdue University

Simmons College
University of California, San Diego
University of New Mexico
University of North Carolina, Chapel Hill
University of West Florida
Wake Forest University

CGS Best Practices in the Responsible Conduct of Research Initiative (NSF, 2006-2008)

Awardee Institutions

Bradley University
Brown University
Old Dominion University
Rockhurst University

University of Alabama at Birmingham
University of Kansas
University of Nebraska, Lincoln
University of Oklahoma

Affiliate Institutions

Appalachian State University
Colorado State University
Duke University
East Carolina University
Florida State University
Georgia Institute of Technology
Indiana University
Middle Tennessee State University
Graduate Studies
Ohio State University
Oklahoma State University

Oregon State University
Pennsylvania State University
Texas State University, San Marcos
University of Colorado, Boulder
University of Idaho
University of Illinois, Urbana-Champaign
University of Maryland, Baltimore County
University of North Carolina, Charlotte
University of Oregon
University of Washington

CGS Graduate Education for the Responsible Conduct of Research (ORI, 2004-2006)

Awardee Institutions

Arizona State University
Duke University
Florida State University
New York Medical College
Old Dominion University

University of Kansas
University of Missouri, Columbia
University of New Hampshire
University of Rhode Island
University of Utah

Affiliate Institutions

Boston College
Chicago School of
   Professional Psychology
Clemson University
Columbia University
Eastern Washington University
Florida International University
Fordham University
Hood College
Howard University
Michigan State University
Purdue University
San Diego State University

Towson University
University of Arkansas
University of Arkansas, Little Rock
University of California, Davis
University of Hawaii, Manoa
University of Illinois, Urbana-Champaign
University of Maryland, Baltimore County
University of Massachusetts, Amherst
University of North Carolina, Chapel Hill
University of North Carolina, Charlotte
University of Wisconsin, Madison
Utah State University
Western Michigan University

Appendix B
Council of Graduate Schools Request for Proposals
The Project for Scholarly Integrity

The Council of Graduate Schools (CGS) is soliciting proposals from CGS member institutions to participate in a collaborative project on scholarly integrity. A new CGS project supported by the Office of Research Integrity (ORI) will award $50,000 to five institutions who will be selected through a competitive process of external review. Participating universities will develop, assess, and disseminate educational models for promoting responsible conduct of research (RCR) and integrity in professional scholarship, education, and research. Participants will share instruments, resources, and models for curricular and administrative integration with each other throughout the project and with the graduate community through CGS meetings and workshops, online resources, and publications. CGS will feature university projects on an enhanced interactive website that will also serve as a clearinghouse of relevant resources and provide electronic forums for exchanging information and advice. As in other CGS best practice initiatives, universities who are not selected to receive awards will be invited to participate as affiliates. A monograph detailing the institutionalization efforts of five major research universities with particular emphasis on what is scalable and transferable to other institutional contexts will be released in conjunction with a capstone conference in October 2010. This culminating event will bring together graduate deans, researchers, corporate leaders, national agencies and private foundations to discuss future trends and showcase best practices in comprehensive institutional approaches to research and scholarly integrity.

I. Project Rationale

In the broader academic context, integrity is a concept rich with connotations that encompass the minimal standards of compliance in research, the personal ethical decision-making processes of individuals, and ultimately the ways in which our institutions reflect the highest aspirations and broadest commitment on the part of the academic profession to the principles of truth, scholarship, and the responsible education of future scholars. Research integrity is not simply an individual value, it is also an institutional value reflected in the culture that is reinforced by the processes in place and the daily decisions of individual researchers, faculty and mentors, campus leaders, and administrative staff. Recent efforts to place greater emphasis on research integrity in graduate education are important in the context of three phenomena: (a) an increase in the number of reported cases of misconduct, nationally and internationally; (b) the encroachment of external pressures upon academic research as interaction and interdependence intensifies among academic, commercial, and government sectors; and (c) the expanding scope of researchers' responsibilities as a consequence of the globalization of the scientific community and the accelerating pace of change. The growing interaction among academic, business, and government sectors and the globalization of the scientific community both have the potential to provide enormous public benefits, but they also mean that the next generation of scholars faces new challenges. What is needed now, more than ever, is for university leaders and scholars to work together to ensure that a strong tradition of research integrity evolves to meet these new challenges. This project represents a continuing collaboration between CGS and member universities on research integrity and is designed to provide models for institutions seeking to take a comprehensive approach to embedding the ethical and responsible conduct of research into the fabric of graduate education.

II. Project Background

This project builds upon two prior CGS pilot projects. An initial project funded by ORI supported the generation and testing of strategic interventions and assessment strategies in the behavioral and biomedical fields at ten universities. The resultant CGS monograph on Graduate Education for the Responsible Conduct of Research focused on program "start up," or the key elements required to launch an effective program. A subsequent NSF-funded CGS initiative supported the integration of RCR into the regular practice of graduate education. That project addressed the needs of students in science and engineering for enhanced skills and competencies in deliberate ethical reasoning about issues that arise in interdisciplinary research and in public-policy arenas. CGS will release the monograph from that project in summer 2008. The project described in this request for proposals builds upon results from both prior projects by drawing on resources created and lessons learned to develop institutional models for expanding and embedding research integrity and responsible conduct of research education programs.

The objectives of this new CGS initiative are: to expand the cadre of graduate deans who will serve as leaders in fostering a climate of research integrity in graduate education; to generate information about what works best in promoting a comprehensive institutional approach to RCR education; to document the results of the funded projects online and in a best practice monograph series; and to promote community-wide activity building on this initiative through publications, frequent meetings, a CGS scholarly integrity Website, and interactive media.

III. Selection Criteria

A selection committee will evaluate proposals based upon the following criteria:

- Institutional Commitment

  - Key leadership of the project by the senior academic officer for graduate education (graduate dean or equivalent) who will serve as principal investigator (PI);
  - Letter of endorsement by president or provost and, where appropriate, senior research administrator;
  - Plan and budget reflecting appropriate allocation of resources needed to initiate the program and to sustain and expand it after the end of the project period;
  - Plan for securing commitment of faculty effort and responsibility to achieve program goals.

- The potential of the project to impact graduate education in the behavioral and biomedical sciences (see also *Eligibility*, p.5).*

---

* In order to ensure meaningful and sustainable improvement in the behavioral and biomedical disciplines chiefly targeted by this initiative, universities may find it important and even necessary to include a forum within the project to involve other fields, such as the humanities and social sciences.

- Quality of action plan to implement a comprehensive, integrated approach to research integrity meeting the requirements in section IV below.
- Ability to develop metrics to measure accomplishment of objectives (see section V below).
- Evidence of innovative ideas for fully integrating the responsible conduct of research into the research environment, as opposed to limiting the presentation of RCR issues into orientation sessions or other activities conducted as an adjunct to the conduct of research and research training.
- Priority will be given to proposals that address the need for improved education in the responsible conduct of research in three core areas of activity:

(1) Interdisciplinary activity
(2) Intercultural activity
(3) Interaction between and among units or groups

IV. Proposal Plan and Activities

Each proposal should present a plan of activities that covers five core areas described below. Each of these areas, as well as questions pertaining to each, should be addressed in every proposal. Proposals should indicate a commitment to the bulleted minimum required activities and address any additional activities that will be undertaken. Innovative approaches are encouraged. [For a more comprehensive list of possible activities, see "The Project for Scholarly Integrity for Graduate Education: A Framework for Collaborative Action" http://www.cgsnet.org/portals/0/pdf/PSI_framework_document.pdf.]

(1) Engage the community in identifying needs.

Key strategies for engaging the graduate community on any improvement initiative are: (a) creating a sense of "vulnerability" linked to opportunity and (b) rewarding excellence in research and education, including mentoring.

Questions:

1. What is the local context on campus for this project? How will the graduate school establish recognition of the local context for the need to promote scholarly integrity through this project?

2. How are proposed activities in this phase of the project designed to encourage recognition of vulnerabilities and/or excellence in research and education?

3. What is your experience with each approach, and why is the proposed approach and respective activities the best for your local institutional context?

(2) Invite key stakeholders to reflect on a plan for action.

- Solicit a clear, public endorsement of the project by senior university leaders.
- Appoint a planning or steering committee.

(3) Act on stakeholder reflections.

Proposals should address how, under the leadership of the senior academic officer for graduate education (graduate dean or equivalent), the design and follow through on a plan for action will involve activities in three areas: a) Content; b) Sequencing of Content and Pedagogy; and c) Collaboration.

a) Content
One of the core features of this project is to encourage approaches that embed, in a rich curriculum, education in the professional standards pertaining to the nine core areas of responsible conduct of research as identified below. This should include focus on skills and competencies in the following areas, as well as bedrock principles and values behind them: 1) Data Acquisition, Management, Sharing, and Ownership; 2) Conflicts of Interest and Commitment; 3) Human Subjects; 4) Animal Welfare; 5) Research Misconduct; 6) Publication Practices and Responsible Authorship; 7) Mentor and Trainee Responsibilities; 8) Peer Review; and 9) Collaborative Research. Other areas that might be considered in a comprehensive approach include: lab management; classroom management and practice; financial stewardship; ethical decision-making and deliberation processes; ethical principles.

Questions:

1. What content areas will your project address? On which areas will it focus, and why?

2. Will your institution be creating new curricular content or adapting existing curricular materials to meet the needs of the local contexts?

3. Where creating new materials, what opportunities will key stakeholders have for providing input into identifying the shortcomings of existing materials and suggesting concrete areas for improvement? Who are the potential collaborators and what are the resources available for this effort?

4. If your project will be adopting and/or adapting existing resources, what are the reasons for choosing the particular curricular content that will be considered?

b) Sequencing of Content and Pedagogy

Projects should move beyond minimal training in proper conduct and professional standards. Aspects to consider include: the sequencing of content to address professional development needs of students and/or to expose students to situations of escalating complexity and encouraging consideration of the broader implications of decisions and deliberations. Institutions proposing to develop original curricular content or to innovate in the area of pedagogy and learning should articulate how proposed activities are grounded in theories of learning.

- Face to face <u>and</u> interactive learning opportunities are an essential requirement of instruction in this project.

Questions:

1. How will content, activities, and resources be sequenced to address the developmental needs of students and/or faculty at appropriate stages in their graduate paths or careers?

2. What pedagogical methods or activities do you anticipate being undertaken or encouraged?

c) Collaboration

- Proposals should identify: key collaborators who will be involved in the project, potential collaborators who will be invited to participate in the project, and the anticipated role for each.

(4) Disseminate to the broader community information about activities and their ongoing impact.

Communication among the leadership group of PI's as well as to the broader CGS community about project achievements is a core requirement. Participation in the following is required:

- Eight PI telephone conferences per year (from September 2008 to September 2010).
- Project sessions convening participants and affiliates at CGS summer and annual meetings (July 2009 to December 2010)
- A capstone conference in October 2010 highlighting project achievements and bringing together key stakeholders from business, government, and non-profit sectors.
- Two face-to-face meetings of graduate deans and affiliates per year (April 2009-August 2010) [*travel expenses paid by CGS; do not include in budgets*].

(5) Integrate curricular and administrative activities, where appropriate, to ensure greatest impact and sustainability.

Proposals should address how curricular resources and content will be integrated into the graduate research experience. Proposals are encouraged to address how administrative processes and procedures may be tuned to reinforce a climate of scholarly integrity. Key considerations should include: sustainability, scalability, and the potential transportability of materials, lessons, and/or resources to other institutions.

Questions:

1. How will resources be developed or adapted to meet the local university context(s)? And what administrative resources will assist in this process?
2. Will curricular content or resources currently serving a small population be scaled up to a larger one?
3. Beyond CGS vehicles for dissemination, how will your institution work to make feasible the transportability of your materials or resources to other universities?

V. Assessment Requirements

Institutions are required to conduct assessment in three areas during the course of the project:

1. Activities assessment
2. The climate for scholarly integrity
3. Student learning

All participants will be required to complete an *activities assessment* using a template provided by CGS: (a) pre-implementation, to be submitted by October 30, 2008, and (b) post-implementation, to be submitted in conjunction with final reports. [Assessment instruments and instructions are available online at: http://www.cgsnet.org.]

Proposals must also indicate a commitment to administering a survey, created by CGS in consultation with PI's, on *the climate for scholarly integrity* within the first six months of receipt of the awards and, again, within the six months period prior to the conclusion of the subaward period. These instruments will be common to participants in the project and will reflect activities in the required areas as well as the elective innovations that universities propose. Support documentation for obtaining campus IRB exemption for survey #2 will be provided by CGS. These assessment instruments will be used to measure the progress of projects over time against their own goals and to gather comparable information across participating institutions about the scope, impact, integration, visibility, and potential sustainability of funded projects.

Projects will also be required to address how *student learning* will be assessed during the course of the project. [Optional student learning assessment tools developed as a result of prior CGS RCR initiatives will be available on the CGS RCR project website, accessible through http://www.cgsnet.org/Default.aspx?tabid=123.]

Beginning in January 2009, CGS project staff will conduct site visits to participating universities.

Eligibility

All U.S. CGS member institutions are eligible to apply for awards. Priority will be given to proposals from institutions that can provide evidence of the project's potential to have a direct and significant impact on behavioral and biological sciences and biomedical research as indicated by the scope of the proposed project (e.g. number of students expected to participate) and relevant national rankings, for example, in receipt of NIH funding.

Reporting Requirements

Annual narrative and financial report due July 30, 2009. Final narrative and financial report due July 30, 2010.

Deadlines

Applications for a CGS/ORI award must be **received at CGS no later than July 30, 2008**. Awards will be announced by September 20, 2008 for projects that will be implemented in September 2008 and conclude in July 2010.

Application Materials

- A proposal (no more than 10 pages, single spaced) outlining proposed activities and demonstrating the applicant institution's ability to meet selection criteria, including a budget specifying the uses for requested funds of $50,000. Indirect costs are not allowable on CGS subawards. (A sample financial reporting form is available upon request if you would like to use this form to structure your budget).
- Letters from departments and faculty demonstrating interest in and commitment to the incorporation of RCR issues into departmental/lab research activities.
- Letter of endorsement by the president or chief academic officer that the activities and intent of the grant are consistent with and complementary to the institutional mission and strategic plans.

Send completed proposals via e-mail (preferred) to: ddenecke@cgs.nche.edu

Proposals sent via U.S. mail will also be accepted (*must be accompanied by an e-mail notice that a proposal is being shipped*):

Council of Graduate Schools
PSI
One Dupont Circle, NW, Suite 230
Washington, DC 20036
www.cgsnet.org

For more information, contact:
Daniel Denecke
ddenecke@cgs.nche.edu
Phone (202) 223-3791
FAX: (202) 331-7157

Appendix C
Final Reports of PSI
Participating Institutions

University of Arizona

CGS Project for Scholarly Integrity
Final Report

Andrew Comrie, Principal Investigator
Associate Vice President for Research, Dean of the Graduate College and
Director of Graduate Interdisciplinary Programs

1. *How did your university define and/or present the core principles underlying your project in communications to its graduate community? (e.g., was the emphasis on "RCR" or responsible conduct of research and research misconduct, "research ethics," or "scholarly integrity"?) What, if any, lessons did your institution learn about communicating the priorities of this project to faculty, students, staff, other stakeholders?*

Defining RCR
RCR was presented to our graduate population as a collective value system comprised of individual research components. These components included the topics of research ethics, scholarly integrity, misconduct, human subjects protection, animal subjects protection, data acquisition, management, sharing, and ownership, mentor/trainee relationships, responsible authorship, peer review, collaborative science, and conflicts of interests.

Presenting RCR as a foundational concept supports our core project objective:

To move research integrity out from the shelter of the compliance office and into the general culture of the university.

Lessons Learned
The time required to manage and deliver communications was underestimated during our project planning stages. Disseminating information throughout any campus community seems to be a universal challenge due to complicated logistics and memo overload. We had to identify less traditional and more creative means of communicating project information such as attending new student orientations and scheduling in-person meetings with key stakeholders. While these options proved to be effective, the supplemental effort did require increased participation from both PI's and the project coordinator.

2. *Please list and briefly describe the activities, interventions and programs implemented on your campus with CGS/ORI award funding (e.g. courses, speaker series, extra-curricular seminars, online training modules, policy revisions, conferences, etc.). Please provide dates and durations of activities and indicate at what stage of your project and how many times they were held.*

Overview of Completed Programs

- University-wide Research Integrity Days conference, including workshops conducted by national and international leaders in research integrity issues;
- Research Integrity Small Grants Program to fund curriculum development, for full courses in RCR and for module development to be incorporated into existing science and methods courses. Funding awards of $500-$1,500 were offered to graduate student/faculty teams.
- Training Events: see tables below.

RCR Training Events – Organized by PIs

Title	Date(s)	Duration	Project Stage	RCR Topics	Frequency	Attendees
1st Annual Research Integrity Days Conference	01/22/2010	7 hrs.	Early stage	Human subjects, authorship, data management, mentor/mentee relationships	Single occurrence	95 grad student/faculty
RCR Workshop	04/23/2010	4 hrs.	Mid stage	Responsible lab practices, conflict of interest, human subjects, animal subjects, research misconduct	1/3 sessions	84 grad students/faculty
RCR Workshop	06/30/2010	4 hrs.	Mid stage	Mentor/mentees, peer review, scientists in today's society, authorship	2/3 sessions	78 grad students/faculty
RCR Workshop	10/22/2010	4 hrs.	Late stage	Interactive Scenarios: Data Acquisition & Management Human Subjects Protection Communications Mentor/Mentee Relationships Identifying Misconduct Policies for Handling Misconduct	3/3 sessions	~40 grad students/faculty

RCR Training Events –Small Grants Programs—Organized by Grad Student Awardees

Title	Date(s)	Duration	Project Stage	RCR Topic	Frequency	Attendees
Workshop Letterpress Posters for Scholarly Integrity	09/25/2010	4 hrs.	Late stage	Authorship, publication	Single occurrence	20 grad students
Workshop Research with Respect: Native American Cultural Heritage	10/02/10	3 hrs.	Late stage	Human subjects, misconduct, data acquisition, publication	Single occurrence	50 grad students
Workshop Life Science Research Integrity	09/08/2010	1.5 hrs.	Mid-stage	Human subjects, animal welfare, misconduct, authorship, data acquisition, conflict of interest, mentor/mentees, publication	Single occurrence	55 grad students
Colloquium: Ethics as Regulation in Linguistic Fieldwork	03/05/2010	1.5 hrs.	Early stage	Human subjects, authorship, data acquisition, peer review	Single occurrence	60 grad students
Panel Collaborative Mapping, Geo-spatial Technologies and the Ethical Conduct of Research	03/05/2010	1.5 hrs.	Early stage	Research misconduct, authorship, data acquisition, conflict of interest, publication.	Single occurrence	150 grad students/faculty
Workshop Community Action Research	04/01/2010	2.5 hrs.	Early stage	Research misconduct, authorship, conflict of interest, mentor/mentees	Single occurrence	25 grad students
Panel The Nature of Light: is Objective Scientific Debate Possible?	04/15/2010–04/18/2010	2 hrs/day	Mid stage	Data acquisition, publication	Single occurrence	30 grad students/faculty

3. *What were some of the most successful activities or programs your university developed, and what contributed to their success? (Please address aspects of administrative coordination if applicable.)*

Small Grants in Research Integrity Program
This was one of the most substantive elements of this project. These awards offset a major barrier to the effective and consistent development of relevant curricular materials—and to the inclusion of such curricula into existing graduate training programs –a lack of support and resources.

The open application process resulted in a multi-disciplinary response across a diverse section of disciplines, which then fosters a centralized awareness of RCR within all aspects of the research environment.

The application requirement for graduate students to partner with faculty members provided opportunities for the direct application of RCR standards in mentoring, authorship, collaborative science, and research integrity.

Most successful activities identified by grant awardees:

- (Graduate students) learning how to plan workshops. Everyone is enthusiastic about the opportunity to be involved.
- Strong student interest in new courses.
- Collaboration with other researchers, identification of many useful resources related to teaching research ethics.
- Collaboration with our partner, the UA Libraries, has been a great success.
- Identifying speakers has been successful.
- A large group of students and faculty heard a controversial speaker and the follow on discussion was enlightening.
- Invited speakers talk well attended, sparked much debate and other, small initiatives.
- Developed and executed new graduate seminar in RCR
- Thinking outside of "standard" research protocol criteria.
- Great Indigenous literature and faculty experience working with Native Nations
- We have had multiple successful events and encounters between students and scholars that have elaborated on the specified RCR themes.
- The proposed workshop was a success. Speakers engaged the graduate student audience in discussion of their work with communities.

- Being able to pilot test course modules with a very active student group.

4. *What were some of the least successful activities developed, and what did your institution learn while trying to conduct them? (Please address aspects of administrative coordination if applicable.)*

Our objective to form a Research Integrity Advisory Group, composed of junior faculty and graduate students, did not materialize to the level we had anticipated. Although we have several faculty and graduate students interested in serving as group members, formal management of this initiative was greatly affected by limits of competing demands on our small-grant PI faculty and graduate students. We did form an ad-hoc advisory group of administrators and senior faculty as part of the small grant review process, and these individuals became engaged in presenting at training workshops. We continue to recognize the importance of engaging regular faculty and graduate students with University administration in development of policy and practice; therefore, the establishment of an advisory group will be a high-priority initiative for 2011.

5. *What were the biggest overall obstacles or challenges that you encountered during your project, and what lessons did your institution learn while confronting them?*

The major obstacles encountered during this project all centered on constraints of time and personnel. Both PI's serve as high-level administrators with active schedules, meaning that they could manage the macro features of the project activities, but it was simultaneously critical that a key staff member (RCR coordinator) had time assigned and was able to monitor and manage day-to-day activities. Furthermore, the level of technical expertise and staff time needed for thorough analysis of climate survey results was not anticipated. Nonetheless, this survey was adopted by the overall group of CGS awardees because of its usefulness in benchmarking and basic information, and it remains a worthwhile extra effort. In short, our plans were ambitious and in large part we achieved them and even exceeded our expectations on some elements. Yet, we also now have a much clearer understanding of the time and effort required for such a wide-ranging and large scale project.

6. *Please indicate which of the following topic areas were covered in the activities listed on question #2. (Provide specific examples where relevant.)*

   a. *Common "core" areas of RCR instruction, such as: human subjects; animal welfare; research misconduct (falsification, fabrication, and plagiarism); authorship; data acquisition, sharing, ownership and management; collaborative scholarship; peer review; conflict of interest and commitment; mentor/mentee responsibilities; publication practices and responsible authorship*
   b. *Other professional standards in the discipline (if applicable)*
   c. *Other professional standards of scholarship and research that transect the discipline*
   d. *Ethical reasoning*
   e. *Ethical theory and/or principles*

   We addressed all of these topic areas, many in considerable detail within the workshops and several in very specialized and focused ways within the small grants. For details, please see the tables in response to question 2.

7. *Please describe any pedagogical methods used in project activities listed on question #2. (For example: case studies, lectures, one-on-one mentoring, on-line self-tutoring, other forms of self-tutoring, discussion groups, on-line discussion groups, team teaching, other).*

   RCR instructional formats have included:

   - Traditional lecture
   - Workshops (scenarios, case studies, role plays and discussion groups)
   - Classroom sessions (Team teaching)
   - Conferences

8. *What recommendations would you give to other institutions planning and/or implementing an RCR program? What would you recommend that other institutions do differently?*

   Review the final PSI grant reports and climate survey results of similar-sized institutions produced by this set of CGS grantee institutions. Although our successes are important benchmarks, be very attentive to the difficulties we faced during this implementation. There are obstacles that can be dealt with as quick fixes prior to a large-scale implementation, and there are challenges that will be constant works in progress. Be sure to identify a clear distinction between the two, address the easy challenges and develop a plan for dealing with more long-term obstacles before introducing an RCR education program. This method of organization should provide a more accurate measure of the time required at all stages of the process.

This type of initiative requires a substantial amount of relationship-building; establish a contact person that can effectively articulate between key stakeholders of differing administrative levels (deans, department heads, grad students, research staff). A strong RCR foundation begins with relationships so be sure this person has ample time for consistent interaction with key stakeholders. In our case, we believe it was particularly valuable that we had an established close collaboration between the Graduate School and the institutional RCR office—in essence, we wanted to do this anyway, and the grant was the catalyst that drove us to expand and broaden our ideas to campus-wide implementation.

9. *For each of the following groups, please provide approximate numbers of participants, campus units (including departments or programs), courses, or resources involved in RCR education:*

a. *Students*: ≈ 406
b. *Faculty*: ≈ 200
c. *Staff*: ≈ 50
d. *Departments*: 52
   Arid Lands Resource Sciences; Arizona Cancer Center; Arizona Center on Aging; Arizona Respiratory Center; Arizona Telemedicine Program; Human Origins Genotyping Laboratory; Biomedical Engineering; College of Public Health; College of Education; College of Nursing; College of Optical Sciences; College of Pharmacy; Dept. of Nursing Research; Dept. of Radiology Research; Electrical and Computer Engineering; Family and Community Medicine; Materials Science and Engineering; Molecular Cardiovascular Research Program; Microbiology; Near Eastern Studies; Nutritional Sciences; Office of Outreach & Multicultural Affairs; College of Medicine; Ophthalmology and Vision Science; Orthopedic Surgery; Pediatric Pulmonary; Pharmaceutical Science; Pharmacology & Toxicology; Physics; Physiology; Plant Sciences; Psychology; Residence Life; Russian

and Slavic Studies; School of Anthropology; School of Geography and Development; School of Information Resources and Library Sciences Sociology; Systems and Industrial Engineering; Cell Biology & Anatomy; Neuroscience; Immunobiology; Chemistry; Entomology; Geosciences; Tree Ring Lab; Hydrology; Computer Science; American Indian Studies; English; Russian; Speech and Hearing; Spanish and Portuguese.

e. *New resources developed (courses, web resources, print materials, campus programs, etc.)*

- o Online RCR course management portal—Desire to Learn (D2L)
- o Research Integrity Days Annual Conference
- o RCR Workshop Series
- o Curricula specific to RCR categories and disciplines
- o RCR education posters
- o Course modules—ethical use of internet resources

10. ***How has your university made use of the collective assessments (Activities and Climate) adopted by the universities in the Project for Scholarly Integrity?***
The Activities assessment was an essential baseline for our understanding of what campus program representatives perceive about RCR. It also provided core benchmark comparisons to other schools that used the instrument. The information we gained was at the college/broad field level, but nonetheless highlighted several potential areas for intervention:

- Develop a strategy for Humanities and Arts (did they ignore the survey because they saw it as not relevant to their field?)
- Provide resources for RCR interpretation/explanation in Health Sciences
- Provide resources for RCR activities/classes in Engineering and Sciences
- Work across campus to add RCR statement/info on all departmental/ program websites
- Provide resources to increase "difficult discussions" in Science and Engineering
- Create programs for postdocs and techs (orientation & in service)
- Originate ways to engage faculty in RCR programs (beyond online training)

The above results, and the administration of our Climate assessment, coincided with the onset of the new NIH and NSF requirements for RCR plans and training on grant applications. We were simultaneously gearing up for campus-wide RCR workshops while being able to apply much of what we learned from the activities assessment, early workshop feedback, and the need to facilitate provision of all kinds of RCR resources for the entire campus. The result was a much more informed and varied set of programming and activities than we would have been able to provide otherwise, given the knowledge and head start that our project provided. We believe we have begun to address all the above areas for intervention, most of them very substantively, in the last 12 months. Certainly, we have been able to provide resources to campus in the culture of RCR and ethics rather than simply responding to the agency mandates in a compliance mentality, and our CGS/ORI PSI project was instrumental in preparing us to do so.

We only received the results of our Climate assessment in the last few months. Our analyses of the broad field results as well as those with break-outs by respondent type have focused on the campus and college-level scales. Overall, they confirm and add value to the Activities assessment results, and underline much of what we knew and what we have learned from other campuses. In the months to come we will take the unit-level results to help us advise individual programs as we start to work on more local-scale implementation of findings. Our principal approach at that level will be outlining and encouraging best practices in disciplinary context.

11. *What material or online resources has your university developed with the use of CGS/ORI award funds (for example, online resources, pedagogical resources, etc.)? Please provide links to online resources below.*

Book Chapter: Successful Research in Indian Country - Respecting the Cultural Integrity and Sovereignty of Native Nations

Videocast: Seminar - Research with Respect: Native American Cultural Heritage

Course Modules: Ethics for Linguistic Fieldwork; Research Integrity in Life Sciences; Responsible and Ethical Research in Indian Country; Research Ethics: Vulnerable Populations in Applied Community Health; Responsible Preservation of Scientific Materials After Publication; Ethical Issues in Internet Research; Ethical Uses of Digital Media.

Poster Series: Research Integrity, Letterpress printed.

Technical Report: The Nature of Light: is Objective Scientific Debate Possible?

Online Multimedia Toolbox:

Main Project Website
Our overall project site is at http://orcr.vpr.arizona.edu/psiaz; this is where we are developing the online RCR library, which is still under construction as our small grant PIs complete their projects and make available the final web resources.

Listed below are a set of presentations from our first Research Integrity Days conference that will be integrated into the online RCR resource library:

Boyce, G.A. The Ethics of Geospatial Research with Politically Vulnerable Populations: an Online Multimedia Toolbox.
http://www.vpr.arizona.edu/system/files/riconfpresent_boyce.pdf

Colombi, B.J., & Van Vlack, K.A. Successful Research in Indian Country: Respecting the Cultural Integrity & Sovereignty of Native Nations
http://www.vpr.arizona.edu/system/files/riconfpresent_colombivanvlack.pdf

Cromey, Doug. The Darkroom is Closed: Image Ethics for a New Generationhttp://orcr.vpr.arizona.edu/system/files/Cromey%20-%20Image%20Ethics%20-%20Jan2010%20-%20handouts.pdf

Grainger, L. A. Strategies for Success: Research Integrity in the Life Sciences Laboratory, A Workshop for First Year Graduate Students
http://www.vpr.arizona.edu/system/files/riconfpresent_grainger.pdf

Hoit, J.D. Mentoring with Integrity
http://www.vpr.arizona.edu/system/files/riconfpresent_hoit.pdf

Rankin, L.L. Yours, Mine, & Ours: The Ethics of Authorship
http://www.vpr.arizona.edu/system/files/riconfpresent_rankin.pdf

Trueman, A.K. Education and Ethics for Field Linguistics
http://www.vpr.arizona.edu/system/files/riconfpresent_trueman.pdf

Online RCR Training Portal

http://d2l.ltc.arizona.edu/d2l/orgTools/ouHome/ouHome.asp?ou=160968

Note: this is not a public site; it is hosted on our campus coursework management system and requires local UA login. It contains a set of modules that will be accessible by faculty and students for use in RCR education and training.

12. *What learning assessment tools has your university used to assess the efficacy of courses, modules, or other pedagogical resources? Have these tools been used to reflect on the efficacy of project activities? If so, how?*

We have used brief surveys to gauge the quality of content included in our RCR Workshop Series. Based on the feedback, participants prefer dynamic instructional formats for RCR education. Thus, our workshop format now includes 10 minutes of subject matter information followed by case studies, group discussions, role plays and other active learning components. Our goal is to provide participants an opportunity to "practice" responses to various compliance situations, resulting in tangible skills that can be applied immediately to actual work/academic environments. Interestingly, this dynamic format represents participant requests, and mirrors best practices in adult learning theory.

We have not used any other formal learning assessment tools to date. However, every course module that is uploaded to our RCR Training Portal will be designed based on best practices in adult learning theory. This format will include assessment tools for each respective module. The consistency in curriculum content and the use of functional assessments will add educational value and institutional credibility to our online RCR training program.

13. *Has your university received feedback from campus groups (graduate students, faculty, staff, or other senior administrators) about the project during and following implementation? What have you learned from this feedback?*

Yes. The feedback has primarily been via assessment surveys following meetings and workshops, with respondents including mainly graduate students and faculty members as well as research staff members. These responses have shaped our programming directly, leading to more hands-on and active-learning modules, even when attendance is large.

The grant was also an excellent vehicle to demonstrate to other senior administrators a tangible example of how the Graduate College and the RCR Office were collaborating in an innovative way.

14. *How important to your university's project was its collaborative activities with other awardee and/or affiliate institutions? What kinds of networks with other universities or model resources (i.e. meetings or workshop sessions with other senior university administrators, models or toolkits, online databases of resources, listservs or chat groups, etc.) would be most useful to universities implementing a similar program?*

These were moderately important. The most important interactions in this arena were the regular meetings of awardees convened by CGS staff. We learned from the experiences of other schools and adopted or adapted ideas to our own situation. Examples include: strategies to promote better assessment completion rates, benchmarking of assessment survey results, expanded exposure to online resources, a forum for discussion of implementation approaches and issues, and the valuable sense of a cohort navigating similar challenges together. Ultimately, the most useful interactions with other universities will be a combination of meetings, conference calls, and a network of networks to coordinate and maximize the set of available resources on our campuses.

15. *Will your university sustain the activities that it implemented during the Project for Scholarly Integrity beyond the period of the CGS/ORI award? Please briefly explain any plans or challenges related to the sustainability of your project.*

Yes, absolutely! We realized from the initial stages that this initiative could not simply be about winning a grant. Instead, it had to be about leveraging our core commitment to creating a new RCR environment on campus.

Our plans are to continue building on the foundation we have put in place. We have excellent baseline and benchmark assessment results to guide a wide set of interventions and adoption of best practices. With this grant our project has produced a key set of locally-produced resources at the disciplinary level, we have developed a cadre of presenters for workshops that can be tuned to individual broad areas or for a general audience, and we have the matching informational references and materials to support all those activities. Our plan is to keep growing the breadth and depth of what we are doing to reach as far as possible into the many varied corners of our campus.

Our challenges are relatively easy ones: personnel time and, to some extent, financial support. Both of these control how rapidly and how far our efforts can reach. Fortunately, we enjoy a strong commitment to excellence in RCR education from the rest of our central administration, without which the job would be much more difficult. Also, we have been well-received by departments and programs who generally seem to appreciate the more upbeat message of us helping them with RCR and ethics education, rather than us forcing a compliance-oriented mentality. With a small number of key staff and a willing group of participating administrators, more staff and as many early-adopters as we can recruit, we are very hopeful about sustaining our efforts into the future.

Columbia University Graduate School of Arts and Sciences

CGS Project for Scholarly Integrity
Final Report

Carlos J. Alonso, Principal Investigator
Acting Dean, Columbia University Graduate School of Arts and Sciences
Jan Allen, Co-P.I.
Associate Dean for Ph.D. Programs

1. **How did your university define and/or present the core principles underlying your project in communications to its graduate community? (e.g., was the emphasis on "RCR" or responsible conduct of research and research misconduct, "research ethics," or scholarly integrity"?) What, if any lessons did your institution learn about communicating the priorities of this project to faculty, students, staff, other stakeholders?**

Columbia's project was designed to address, and communicated to, as broad an audience as possible. We included responsible conduct of research (RCR) to capture the interest and needs of those primarily in the natural sciences and empirical social sciences. We included scholarly integrity to capture the needs of those in the humanities and social sciences. We also included a focus on ethics and responsible conduct in teaching, which crosses all departments and disciplines. This broad approach was designed to create awareness and conversations across all of Columbia's audiences and programs. One drawback to this approach was that in some cases efforts seemed too general or generic to capture specific audiences. Another drawback was that with a small leadership and implementation team, the momentum was slower than we would have liked. It was not possible to have an activity or program each week or each month that would attract audiences from all disciplines and departments. Another lesson learned relates to our goal to move to required RCR/SI training for all Columbia Ph.D. students. Although this would be a graduate school-wide requirement, we would move forward only after having a comprehensive plan for shared leadership with the provost's office and the school deans.

2. **Please list and briefly describe the activities, interventions and programs implemented on your campus with CGS/ORI award funding (e.g., courses, speaker series, extra-curricular seminars, online training modules, policy revisions, conferences, etc.). Please provide dates and durations of activities and indicate at what stage of your project and how many times they were held.**

Central programming (workshops) offered throughout the project period

- The Immortal Life of Henrietta Lacks, with author Rebecca Skloot, February 2, 2010 (1½-hour)
- On Being An Expert: Using Your Research in Consulting and Courtrooms, April 28, 2010 (1-hour)
- Doing the Right Thing: What Every Graduate Student Should Know about Research Misconduct, April 13, 2010; September 29, 2010 (1-hour)
- Who Owns Your Research? Intellectual Property Issues, September 27, 2010 (1-hour)
- Issues in International Research, October 4, 2010 (1-hour)
- The Art, Science, and Ethics of Negotiation, March 30, 2010; June 15, 2020
- Responsibility and Social/Electronic Media, September 30, 2010 (1-hour)
- Financial, Intellectual, and Other Conflicts of Interests, TBA (1½-hour)
- Responsible Publishing Practices, November 15, 2010 (1-hour)

Departmental Conferences
Dealing with Human Remains in Research, Anthropology, Spring 2011
Ethical Issues in Disability Studies Literature and Research, English, Spring 2011

Departmental Needs Assessment/Open Forum meetings
Applied Physics and Applied Mathematics, March 3, 2010 (1½-hour)
Biological Sciences, February 4, 2010 (2-hours)
Cellular, Molecular, and Biophysical Studies, February 18, 2010 (1-hour)
Chemistry, February 16, 2010 (1½-hour)
English, November 17, 2010
Neurobiology, February 4, 2010 (2-hours)
Political Science, February 12, 2010 (1-hour)

And two departmental meetings to be completed in 2010-2011
Anthropology
Sociology

3. **What were some of the most successful activities or programs your university developed, and what contributed to their success? (Please address aspects of administrative coordination if applicable.)**

The most successful activities were the needs assessment/open forum lunch discussions that lead to creating departmental training and to workshops in our FIRST series. Students and post-docs valued the opportunity to share their experiences, especially with each other. On many occasions and across several departments, student comments were met by this response from other students: "I didn't know this was also an issue in your lab." "I have that same problem with my advisor." "Why have we not talked about this in the department before?" Whether students believe it is inappropriate to ask questions (several students told us that asking a question sounded too much like questioning their advisor) or whether the RCR/PSI topics prompt conversations that are especially sensitive or circumstances in which students feel particularly vulnerable, students and post-docs reported that the opportunity to talk among themselves about RCR/PSI topics was especially valuable. (Students from one science department told us: "If the project does nothing more than bring us together on a regular basis to talk to each other, it will have been successful.")

The central programming was successful in that students from various disciplines discovered that they shared some of the same problems and concerns (e.g., about mentoring, authorship practices); on many occasions students shared solutions that worked in one program for possible use in another. We also found this to be one of the successes of each meeting of our advisory board: Faculty and officers whose expertise was in an area of RCR/PSI training, research, or compliance often were sharing ideas and resources with others who had the same role and responsibilities but within the silo of their own school or program. We considered that fact that advisory board meetings often lasted well beyond the scheduled time and agenda as board members continued the conversation to be a mark of success—not inefficiency or poor time management.

4. **What were some of the least successful activities developed, and what did your institution learn while trying to conduct them? (Please address aspects of administrative coordination if applicable.)**

When we define "least successful" as those activities that generated less interest and participation, then there are two project components: the minigrants we offered to departments to plan and provide department-specific

RCR/SI training (up to $5,000) and the mini-grants we offered to faculty to create new graduate RCR courses or (more likely) to revise an existing graduate course to include an emphasis on RCR/SI training (up to $1,000). We had three departments, and two faculty, respond to our Request for Proposals. We funded all these requests. We think it's possible that re-advertising the availability of this funding now that the project is well under way and there is greater awareness of our effort may result in more departmental and faculty response. (We plan to do this with the extension through end of March for use of project funds.)

5. **What were the biggest overall obstacles or challenges that you encountered during your project, and what lessons did your institution learn while confronting them?**

    - Our biggest challenge was, and to some degree remains, how to engage faculty in RCR/PSI training. It is clear that students want to receive information and guidance from their advisors, P.I.s, and other faculty in their discipline and program. It is clear that many faculty believe they are modeling the behaviors that students should emulate and that specific training on these issues is unnecessary, or at best, should be minimal i.e., time spent in the lab or in the archives or writing the dissertation is encouraged, valued, and rewarded. Students perceive their situation and environment as being very different from the circumstances in which faculty operate. Based on our conversations with students, they report having more pressure, fewer resources, and obviously much less information than faculty do. They also perceive the consequences of any kind of failure—ethical, research, academic —as being much greater for students than for faculty. Structurally, we in the graduate school work directly with the Directors of Graduate Studies and not so much with other faculty. Our goal going forward is to increase the involvement and engagement of the Offices of the Provost and the Vice President for Arts and Sciences in our RCR/PSI efforts with an emphasis on more faculty engagement with incentives and rewards for doing so.
    - We were intrigued by student response to our central programming: Some students in the humanities thought the programming was too science-focused; some students in the sciences perceived the very same programming as more focused on the humanities. We learned that students want the workshop and discussion topics to be very focused on the

specific circumstances they find themselves in. Several students told us: "Don't use the term 'ethics' in your workshop titles; that is too generic. We won't come to workshops about ethics!" Instead they see their time better spent at events that help them solve the problems they were having with their advisors: how to talk to advisors who had not explained the lab's authorship policy or how to address concerns when faculty ask students to provide peer review of manuscripts without offering guidance or training and without acknowledging the work of the students. Students want just-in-time information (an ethics hotline?) to help them with immediate dilemmas so they can return to the lab and to the library as quickly as possible.

6. **Please indicate which of the following topic areas were covered in the activities listed on question #2. (Provide specific examples where relevant.)**

   a. **Common core areas of RCR instruction, such as human subjects, animal welfare, research misconduct (falsification, fabrication, and plagiarism); authorship; data acquisition, sharing, ownership and management; collaborative scholarship; peer review; conflict of interest and commitment; mentor/mentee responsibilities; publication practices and responsible authorship.** We included all these topics.

   b. **Other professional standards in the discipline (if applicable).** In our session titled Responsible Publishing Practices, we included standards of the professional journals for authorship determination. And at other sessions, we provided a resource to students that listed the code of ethical conduct for the major professional societies.

   c. **Other professional standards of scholarship and research that transect the discipline.** No.

   d. **Ethical reasoning.** We recently asked two faculty members in Columbia's philosophy department and Teachers College's Philosophy and Education department to develop and present a workshop for us on understanding the ethical and cognitive reasoning skills of our undergraduate students vis-à-vis teaching them the importance of avoiding research misconduct and plagiarism.

   e. **Ethical theory and/or principles.** No.

7. **Please describe any pedagogical methods used in project activities listed on question #2. (For example: case studies, lectures, one-on-one mentoring, on-line self-tutoring, other forms of self-tutoring, discussion groups, on-line discussion groups, team teaching, other).**

    We used open forum discussion groups, workshops presented by our GSAS staff, presentations by guest speakers, moderated panel of faculty speakers, and RCR/PSI case studies (introduced as a new activity in our Preparing Future Faculty sessions).

8. **What recommendations would you give to other institutions planning and/or implementing an RCR program? What would you recommend that other institutions do differently?**

    *   Think comprehensively, but start small. Develop your long-term goals and objectives for the project so that multiple ideas, resources, partners, and audiences are in play. But consider selecting just a few departments (such that they can represent broader discipline clusters such as sciences, social sciences, and humanities) and develop discipline-specific, department-specific models. Seek depth in a few departments rather than breadth across many departments in the beginning. These early program efforts provide models of what works and what doesn't; and they also can provide advocates and consultants as you begin to work with additional departments.
    *   Move beyond survey needs assessment. When we began to conduct the RCR/PSI Activities Training Inventory, several departments reported that they "didn't know how they would complete the inventory." We offered to meet with the Director of Graduate Studies (DGS) and the Academic Department Administrator (ADA) and talk through/ walk through the Inventory questions. These conversations resulted in some of the richest, most revealing information about department climate and culture for RCR/PSI training. Similarly, when we first started our project, we met, department by department, with graduate students and post-doctoral fellows in an open forum discussion over lunch. We asked one question: "About which RCR/PSI topics do you wish you could have more conversations in the department?" The resulting discussion never lasted less than hour as the students and post-docs talked about the department culture and their need for information. They made it clear they wanted these conversations to

occur with their advisors/P.I.s. And they were equally adamant that the mentors should know to initiate these conversations to provide the information students wanted rather than waiting for students to ask.

- Involve skilled facilitators in these discussions. Once we learned how useful it was to conduct additional needs assessment through face-to-face meetings and conversation, it helped to have someone who could guide groups of students and post-docs, as well as DGSs and ADAs, in conversations without fear of "airing the department's dirty laundry," of the information being repeated or reported in inappropriate ways, or of consequences and retribution.
- Do what Michigan State did: Get your president and provost involved early so that visible involvement and leadership come from the highest levels.
- Funding to support your efforts helps. But if no cost or low cost activities are all the institution can afford, don't despair. You will find among your faculty, students, and post-docs those who will champion the cause of RCR/PSI training without requiring tangle rewards. Find these advocates and let them lead.

9. **For each of the following groups, please provide approximate numbers of participants, campus units (including departments or programs), courses, or resources involved in RCR education:**

   a. **Students**
   b. **Faculty**
   c. **Staff**
   d. **Departments (please list)**
   e. **New resources developed (courses, web resources, print materials, campus programs, etc.)**

We provide conservative estimates of (a), (b), and (c) above as we report total unique participants, not total attendance. We hope that some of our post-project assessments will help us learn whether, for example, our student participants returned to their lab or advisors and asked questions or continued a discussion of topics from our training workshops. Time and time again students told us that they wanted to hear this information from their advisors in the context of their own research and scholarship (and not necessarily from a discussion of "famous and infamous cases" of research misconduct.)

a. Students—We had 728 students attending our departmental and central training events. We advertised our events to a total of 3,445 Ph.D. students, 5,337 master's students, and 798 post-doctoral fellows.

b. Faculty—We worked directly with 59 Directors of Graduate Study and 18 additional faculty members in our project.

c. Staff—We had no direct participation by staff, such as research technicians, in our activities. (They were included in our climate research survey.)

d. Departments (please list)
   Anthropology
   Applied Physics and Applied Mathematics
   Biological Sciences
   Cellular, Molecular, and Biophysical Studies
   Chemistry
   English
   Neurobiology
   Political Science
   Sociology

e. New resources developed (courses, web resources, print materials, campus programs, etc.)—We developed a web site that included existing resources but developed no new resources yet. We prepared hand-outs of information and recommended resources for most of our workshops (presented by GSAS rather than by guest speakers). In 2009-2010 and 2010-2011 we developed and presented 14 new training workshops, hosted two outside speakers, and funded two disciplinary conferences (to take place spring 2011). We hosted nine departmental open forum meetings with graduate students and post-doctoral fellows. Our two faculty mini-grants resulted in new materials for two courses.

10. **How has your university made use of the collective assessments (Activities and Climate) adopted by the universities in the Project for Scholarly Integrity?**

Columbia made use of the RCR/PSI Activities Training Inventory in two primary ways: We used it for project planning purposes to select departments and identify training topics for our initial efforts. Also, when Columbia's

Office of Research, Division of Research Compliance Education, began to identify existing resources at Columbia that would help trainees meet the new NSF RCR training requirement, OR/RCE found our RCR/PSI Activities Training Inventory to be the most comprehensive survey available of central, school, and departmental RCR training. We have not yet used the Climate Survey results. (The Michigan State/Penn State/Wisconsin consortium provides a stellar model. Their 50 percent response rate, compared with Columbia's less than 20 percent rate, suggests that we must use our results in ways less comprehensive and comparative among departments.

11. **What materials or online resources has your university developed with the use of CGS/ORI award funds (for example, online resources, pedagogical resources, etc.)? Please provide links to online resources below.**

We have not yet developed new online resources as part of our project. Our PSI web site provides a link to existing resources that can be used by faculty and other trainers.

http://www.columbia.edu/cu/gsas/sub/project/research/main/.

12. **What learning assessment tools has your university used to assess the efficacy of courses, modules, or other pedagogical resources? Have these tools been used to reflect on the efficacy of project activities? If so, how?**

We have used one other learning assessment tool (provided in our original proposal) as a pre-project assessment of (1) students' perception of the importance of various RCR/PSI topics to their success as a researcher/scholar and (2) their perception of their knowledge level of the topic. This information helped us in planning our training topics. We will do a post-training assessment with the same instrument, likely in summer 2011, to measure any changes in student assessment of the importance of RCR/PSI topics and student perception of their knowledge.

13. **Has your university received feedback from campus groups (graduate students, faculty, staff, or other senior administrators) about the project during and following implementation? What have you learned from this feedback?**

During the last month of our project we met again with our advisory board and our Research Ethics Fellows (who have worked with us to plan department- and discipline-specific programming). Their feedback reinforces our belief that, although our central programming promoted discussion of RCR/PSI issues in interdisciplinary ways, trainees want their P.I.s and advisors to engage in discussion about very specific and real issues trainees face in their research and scholarship (as opposed to having speakers and "ethics experts" present training workshops). Going forward we want to create more faculty involvement through enhanced opportunities, incentives, and rewards.

14. **How important to your university's project was its collaborative activities with other awardee and/or affiliate institutions? What kinds of networks with other universities or model resources (i.e. meetings or workshop sessions with other senior university administrators, models or toolkits, online databases of resources, listservs or chat groups, etc.) would be most useful to universities implementing a similar program?**

We at Columbia acknowledge how much we relied on other awardee colleagues as they shared their ideas for project activities and resources. Our location in New York City also provides a special opportunity for collaboration: We have three other educational institutions literally across the street. Barnard College, Teachers College, and Union Theological Seminary are affiliated institutions with Columbia, and their faculty and students were invited to participate in our project activities. This current academic year (2010-2011) we invited graduate students from an additional four institutions within the city (Fordham, New York University, New School, Stony Brook) to participate in our activities. We plan to continue and extend this collaboration to joint planning and hosting of RCR/PSI activities. Other universities, when not located close enough for joint activities, could find useful collaborations via online means, such as listservs, web resources, video, or Skype broadcast of programming.

15. **Will your university sustain the activities that it implemented during the Project for Scholarly Integrity beyond the period of the CGS/ORI award? Please briefly explain any plans or challenges related to the sustainability of your project?**

Our response to this question is **without a doubt!** Although the pace at which we developed and conducted our project activities up to this point is directly attributable to our project proposal schedule and the encouragement and innovative models provided by our colleagues at the other PSI institutions, we are continuing the three most successful components of our project: (1) the needs assessment lunch-time meetings with graduate students and post-docs in each graduate program, which form the basis for (2) our discipline- and department-specific workshops, and (3) the FIRST workshop series that is open to students and post-docs from all graduate programs at Columbia and its affiliated institutions: Teachers College, Union Theological Seminary, and Barnard College. We also plan to continue to work with our Directors of Graduate Studies, the Executive Committee of the Graduate School of Arts and Sciences (ECGSAS), and our Advisory Board to promote greater faculty involvement in RCR training and engagement in RCR mentoring with their trainees.

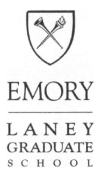

EMORY
LANEY
GRADUATE
SCHOOL

CGS Project for Scholarly Integrity
Final Report

Lisa A. Tedesco, Principal Investigator
Vice Provost for Academic Affairs, Graduate Studies and Dean of the James
T. Laney School of Graduate Studies

1. **How did your university define and/or present the core principles under-
    lying your project in communications to its graduate community? (e.g.,
    was the emphasis on "RCR" or responsible conduct of research and re-
    search misconduct, "research ethics," or "scholarly integrity"?) What, if
    any, lessons did your institution learn about communicating the priorities
    of this project to faculty, students, staff, other stakeholders?**

In the Laney Graduate School's (LGS) proposal and subsequent Project
for Scholarly Integrity (PSI), principles and activities were communicated
with emphasis on research ethics and scholarly integrity. The guiding principles of the Emory proposal were:

1. **Program integration.** Education in research ethics and integrity must
    be integrated into the curriculum of the student's program.
2. **Critical reflection.** The pedagogy of research ethics must develop the
    student's skills of critical reflection on the complicated problems of
    professional integrity.
3. **Knowledge of standards, regulations, and best practices.** Students
    must have a clear understanding of what the law, professional codes of
    ethics, and best practices in the discipline demand of them.

At the onset of the Project, the LGS assembled a steering committee to help plan initial programming and to raise campus-wide awareness about the project. The steering committee was composed of faculty and administrators from across the campus including the School of Medicine, the Emory Center for Ethics and the Office of Research. LGS rolled the project out campus-wide in the fall of 2009. We worked through program leadership by briefing the Directors of Graduate Studies about the goals of the program and planned events. In the spring semester of 2010, we created a faculty and graduate student working group to begin shaping the program. This group elaborated the guiding principles of the proposal into more specific program values and intended outcomes. This latter list was disseminated to the DGS's, and shared with faculty and graduate students at a series of Open Forums in the fall semester of 2010.

One of the challenges we confronted was that understanding of the need for RCR/SI was uneven across the University. In the natural sciences and some social science programs, for example, the need for training in research ethics was driven, in part, by the requirements of external funding agencies such as the National Science Foundation and National Institutes of Health that now require such training of all funding recipients. For the humanities and some social sciences, the perceived need for research ethics training was much less urgent. LGS depends upon the assistance of its graduate programs to disseminate the priorities of graduate education to students and other stakeholders. For this reason, targeted messaging, coupled with a broad rollout, might have been a better way to develop traction at an earlier stage of project development.

A positive lesson from our experience is that *engagement* with the principles is more important than *communication* of them. We began with a small number of broad principles. The program principles with which we are going forward arose out of faculty and graduate student discussions that were part of our Project for Scholarly Integrity. We feel that there is substantial buy-in to the principles because they were developed in collaboration with the community.

2. **Please list and briefly describe the activities, interventions and programs implemented on your campus with CGS/ORI award funding (e.g. courses, speaker series, extra-curricular seminars, online train-**

**ing modules, policy revisions, conferences, etc.). Please provide dates
and durations of activities and indicate at what stage of your project
and how many times they were held.**

In the early stages of the project, fall 2009, PIs and the PSI Steering Committee
worked to conceptualize and launch the speaker series *Beyond Right & Wrong:
Engaging Ethics at Emory*. For each event (except the first), a multidisciplinary
group of faculty, researchers and students were recruited to participate in panel
discussions with featured guests. Topics of these events included:

o October 7, 2009: *Research Integrity: National Issues, Local Challenges*, which featured guest Tina Gunsalus (University of Illinois,
   Urbana-Champaign)
o November 18, 2009: *Scholarly Misconduct: What is it? Why it Matters? What Can be Done to Eliminate It?* featuring Dr. Nicholas Steneck (University of Michigan)
o March 3, 2010: *Animals in Research* with Dr. Gary Comstock (North
   Carolina State University)
o April 20, 2010: *The Truth, the Whole Truth and Nothing But the Truth:
   Is Scholarly Integrity Still Possible?* with Dr. Greg Koski (Harvard
   Medical School)

In October 2009, also in the first stages of the project, LGS issued a call
for proposals to faculty and graduate students. Coupled with the launch
of the *Beyond Right & Wrong* speaker series, LGS sought to support several kinds of enterprises. Proposals were accepted for the development of
course and course materials as well as events such as workshops, lectures
or performances that promoted the discussion of RCR. Of the proposals
received, the LGS decided to fund four: one for a faculty member who
seeking to develop a course for graduate students on the teaching of ethics;
a second for a post-doctoral student to develop an *ethics book club*; and
a third from a humanities graduate student seeking to develop a *Research
Ethics Roundtable* to discuss books, articles and topics in RCR. Finally,
we funded a student-generated event featuring author Rebecca Skloot (*The
Immortal Life of Henrietta Lacks*).

In Spring 2010, as the project moved to the next phase of development,
LGS assembled a multidisciplinary *Program Working Group* that convened
over two meetings. The first meeting provided project background and doc-

umentation around existing Emory activities (gleaned from the Inventory) and RCR/ethics program models at other institutions such as Duke, Florida State, Notre Dame, Penn State, Princeton, Purdue, University at Buffalo, State University of New York and University of Missouri-Columbia.

For the second meeting, Working Group members were asked to be prepared with ideas for programming and model structures for RCR/SI education at Emory. A lively discussion generated a number of ideas. There was consensus on the broad outlines of a program.

Based upon the array of suggested models presented by Working Group members, project PIs synthesized the group's ideas into three models and then sought comments from the Working Group and LGS staff. Discussions with these groups and members of the Emory Center for Ethics led PIs to forego presenting the three models directly to faculty and students and to instead provide faculty and students with some principles and values as well as pedagogical goals to be included in any model of programming adopted by the LGS and integrated into PhD studies here at Emory:

Principles and Values

- Each student should receive substantial and substantive education in all areas of RCR/SI relevant to his/her research and career path.
- RCR/SI education should be integrated into PhD study; it should be an organic part of a PhD program
- Students should have some experiences where different disciplines discuss ethical questions together, so that disciplinary similarities and differences can be identified.
- RCR/SI education should be dispersed throughout a student's career, so that questions are encountered when they are meaningful and timely.
- Faculty from a student's program should be involved in discussion of ethical questions, especially those specific to the discipline.
- RCR/SI education should be tracked on the student's transcript.
- There should be regular, systematic assessment of RCR/SI educational programming

Pedagogical Goals
- Emory PhDs will be able to disentangle the elements of a complex ethical problem and to reason about them so as to arrive at fair and just solutions.

- Emory PhDs will have the communication skills necessary to prevent ethical conundrums, and resolve them when they arise.
- Emory PhDs will know the disciplinary codes of conduct or legal mandates relevant to their field.
- Emory PhDs will receive certification in those areas where certification is necessary (e.g. IRB training).
- Emory PhDs will be familiar with the resources for resolving ethical problems, and know how to report misconduct when it occurs.

In the fall semester of 2010, the LGS is hosting several open forums to discuss the formal integration of training in the responsible conduct of research and scholarly integrity into PhD studies here at Emory. Discussion will begin with a presentation of the above principles and goals. On the basis of these discussions, the Working Group will design an LGS-wide program and present it to LGS faculty and administrative leadership in the spring semester of 2011.

3. **What were some of the most successful activities or programs your university developed, and what contributed to their success? (Please address aspects of administrative coordination if applicable.)**

The speaker series, *Beyond Right & Wrong: Engaging Ethics at Emory*, was a resounding success. Attendees at every event included a healthy mix of faculty, researchers and students from across disciplines, though mostly concentrated in the natural and social sciences. The presenters invited to headline these events were widely known, respected and knowledgeable in all areas of research and scholarly integrity. These speakers were also able to meet individually with LGS administration as well as faculty and students to discuss their own work and ways that Emory might move its project forward. For each visit, time was also set aside to meet with members of the advisory committee and working groups for open discussion on how to advance broad institutional engagements, practices, and commitments for PSI/RCR.

LGS also found success in the Working Group. When charged with reviewing existing RCR programs at other institutions and then coming together to brainstorm what might work at Emory, the group responded with creative and thoughtful model ideas that have since informed all outreach to faculty, students and leadership across campus. The Working Group will meet again in the coming weeks following the open forums to discuss received feed-back and ideas and to help formulate a model that LGS can bring before the faculty and governing bodies of LGS. Having faculty and stakeholders take a hands-on role in developing this program has allowed LGS to move forward with ambassadors who are able to discuss the program with fellow faculty and students as crafters of its design. This will be invaluable as LGS moves to integrate the program into the graduate curriculum here at Emory.

4. **What were some of the least successful activities developed, and what did your institution learn while trying to conduct them? (Please address aspects of administrative coordination if applicable.)**

The goals of Phase 1 of the project were to raise awareness of ethical issues and vulnerabilities and to begin discussions of how best to prepare graduate students to think through ethical questions. While these goals were met, we did so in ways slightly different from what we anticipated in the original proposal. To raise awareness and begin discussion, we proposed a series of public events. Some of these were to originate from the LGS, and others were to be seeded with mini-grants. We found, however, that there was less perceived need for discussion of research ethics than we anticipated. Our call for mini-grants generated several interesting and exciting proposals, but the response rate was lower than we had hoped. We also tried to host three town-hall meetings in the fall semester of 2009 where we could have an open discussion of the challenges and opportunities of teaching RCR/SI. Attendance was very low, and the meetings attracted those who had recent experience with highly charged events, rather than the broader community we hoped to reach. These two experiences led us to change our approach. We took the initiative by inviting several high-profile speakers. To reach out to the faculty and graduate students, we assembled discussion panels around the speakers. These events were well attended and provoked lively discussion. By the middle of the spring 2010 semester, we had identified a number of faculty and graduate students who were interested in participating in the Project for Scholarly Integrity. The Open Forums being held during the fall 2010 semester, by contrast, are much better attended and have engendered lively discussion. We regard this change in community interest to be sparked by two factors. First, panelists who were invited to participate in the speaker series and members of the Working Group have seeded interest in the graduate programs. Second, the speaker series reached a larger, more diverse audience and signaled that the LGS is taking RCR/SI seriously.

5. **What were the biggest overall obstacles or challenges that you encountered during your project, and what lessons did your institution learn while confronting them?**

As previously discussed, establishing project traction took more time than initially planned. Symptoms of this were the low response to the LGS call for mini-grants and lower than expected participation in the first round of town-hall meetings. LGS corrected this course through adding panels to the speaker series and the creation of the Working Group, and we have experienced a greater response in our fall 2010 Open Forums.

Phase 2 of the original proposal aimed at developing curricular capacity and Phase 3 sought to develop a systematic program of RCR/SI education and integrate it into the curricula of all LGS programs. As a result of our conversations with faculty and graduate students, and the discussions at the *Beyond Right & Wrong* events, it became clear that we had made assumptions about how faculty interest would grow. The different constituencies in the graduate faculty and students reflected a wide variety of assumptions and priorities. To move toward formulating the shape of the overall LGS program, we established the working group of faculty and graduate students. As previously described, this group originated several program ideas as well as guiding principles and pedagogical goals. As faculty and graduate students begin to understand the different ways that the program might take shape, the curricular needs will become clear.

In essence, our experiences showed that Phase 2 and Phase 3 could not be pursued independently. As we refine the program and build consensus (Phase 3), we will also begin preparing course content and developing faculty resources (Phase 2). Toward this latter end, we will be redirecting the mini-grants and the faculty development resources in the original budget to curriculum development and training. We are using CGS funds to begin two projects that will be continued after the grant period ends.

First, we will develop a database of recommended course materials, including readings, syllabi, video, role plays, and so on. Beginning in the spring of 2010, LGS staff culled through some of the vast amount of literature on RCR/SI and collected materials that were pedagogically appropriate for the Emory context. The next phase of development, to be completed this year, will be to further winnow the material and collect it around each of the nine RCR areas (and others as needed). We plan to make funds available to a small number of faculty and graduate students who will use their expertise to assemble teaching resources. The goal is to make available easily usable blocks of pedagogical material.

Second, we have begun planning for a first train-the-trainer workshop to be given in the summer of 2011. One of our primary goals is to develop a program that focuses on ethical problem solving, and the pedagogy of ethical reasoning is quite different from the pedagogy of compliance. The goal of this seminar will be to familiarize faculty with ways of teaching ethics that facilitates open-ended discussions and a safe space for reflection without leaving the impression that "anything goes."

6. **Please indicate which of the following topic areas were covered in the activities listed on question #2. (Provide specific examples where relevant.)**

    a. **Common "core: areas of "RCR" instruction, such as: human subjects; animal welfare; research misconduct (falsification, fabrication, and plagiarism); authorship; data acquisition, sharing, ownership and management; collaborative scholarship; peer review; conflict of interest and commitment; mentor/mentee responsibilities; publication practices and responsible authorship**
    b. **Other professional standards in the discipline (if applicable)**
    c. **Other professional standards of scholarship and research that transect the discipline**
    d. **Ethical reasoning**
    e. **Ethical theory and/or principles**

Speaker Series: Beyond Right & Wrong: Engaging Ethics at Emory

- October 7, 2009: *Research Integrity: National Issues, Local Challenges*, which featured guest Tina Gunsalus (University of Illinois, Urbana-Champaign)

    o   core issues addressed included data management, falsification and ownership, research misconduct, publication practices and conflict of interest

- November 18, 2009: *Scholarly Misconduct: What is it? Why it Matters? What Can be Done to Eliminate It?* featuring Dr. Nicholas Steneck (University of Michigan)

  o core issues addressed included all core areas of RCR as well as ethical reasoning]

- March 3, 2010: *Animals in Research* with Dr. Gary Comstock (North Carolina State University)

  o core issues addressed included animals in research, research misconduct and ethical reasoning/principles

- April 20, 2010: *The Truth, the Whole Truth and Nothing But the Truth: Is Scholarly Integrity Still Possible?* with Dr. Greg Koski (Harvard Medical School)

  o core issues addressed included research misconduct, collaborative scholarship, publication practices/responsible authorship and mentor/mentee responsibilities as well as ethical reasoning and principles]

Call for Proposals for the Awarding of Mini-Grants
Proposals were accepted for the development of course and course materials as well as events such as workshops, lectures or performances that promoted the discussion of RCR. Of the proposals received, LGS decided to fund four:

- Development of a course in the Ethics of Teaching

  o Emory takes the ethics of teaching to be an important area of scholarly integrity, in addition, this course will discuss plagiarism, conflict of interest, and mentoring

- Research Ethics Roundtable

  o Plagiarism, authorship, publication practices

- Ethics book club

- o Open ended, depending on participant's decisions. Potentially all areas of RCR

- Seminar and public lecture featuring author Rebecca Skloot (*The Immortal Life of Henrietta Lacks*)

- o Human subject research, ethical responsibility of scientists to the public

7. **Please describe any pedagogical methods used in project activities listed on question #2. (For example: case studies, lectures, one-on-one mentoring, on-line self-tutoring, other forms of self-tutoring, discussion groups, on-line discussion groups, team teaching, other).**

Events of the *Beyond Right & Wrong* speaker series featured invited guests who would present upon a specific topic for half an hour or so before joining a moderated panel discussion with Emory faculty and researchers and finally, fielding questions from the audience. These events thus involved both lecturing and discussion.

The featured guest of the inaugural speaker series event, Tina Gunsalus, also hosted a workshop for Emory faculty on *whistleblowing in data management* where she used role-play exercises to work through faculty and student responses to ethical dilemmas.

The course on the ethics of teaching, the roundtable and the book club involved discussion.

8. **What recommendations would you give to other institutions planning and/or implementing an RCR program? What would you recommend that other institutions do differently?**

There were three lessons that we learned from the activities supported by CGS.

First, awareness of the need for RCR training and education is uneven across the university. In any planning, priority must be given to raising awareness of RCR/SI issues and their importance for graduate education. Lecture and public events are useful, but must be supplemented by data about local attitudes and resources. The *climate survey* can be useful for identifying global attitudes and areas within the university that could need attention. At Emory, the total population surveyed was rather small, in comparison to the larger programs, like at Penn State, Michigan State and Wisconsin. Our response rate was on the respectable side of small, as well, about 20%. To get more powerful analyses, we combined programs into their divisions (natural science, social science, and humanities). Viewed at this level, there were no stark deficiencies according to the climate survey. In this format, the climate survey gave us very little traction in discussion with particular programs. We will perform another round of analyses with advice from statistical consultants to see if legitimate weighted comparisons for responses by category provide further distinctions that might shape future programming. In addition, it is noted that the some technical matters on the Penn State side delayed the administration of our survey. When it was finally administered, it was well after our PSI/RCR project announcements and kick off events. The *CGS inventory* helped identify both needs and some resources of which we were not aware. In the fall of 2010, we conducted a second survey that focused on the specific RCR areas that are currently included in course offerings. This provided an interesting, finer-grained snapshot of current practices. It was informative about specific gaps, and helped motivate graduate program leadership to expand their coverage and participate in the planning of a university-wide scholarly integrity program.

Second, we demonstrated that there has to be a dynamic interaction between the development of an overall program and the development of the course content. In addition, this dynamism is fed by the growing awareness of need mentioned above. As faculty and graduate students become aware of the need for RCR/SI education, they can begin to see what kind of program the Laney Graduate School needs to implement, and on that basis they can survey their own resources and develop programming that meets their perceived needs.

Finally, it is essential to respect faculty and student time. Faculty and graduate students already feel overloaded and do not welcome the addition of additional coursework or requirements. A clear, data-driven picture of what is already being offered (in our case, generated by both the CGS inventory and our own) was necessary for faculty and graduate students to get a sense of how much they are already doing to teach scholarly integrity. Insofar as the overall program fills a perceived need, the faculty and graduate students will be motivated to develop the additional course content.

9. **For each of the following groups, please provide approximate numbers of participants, campus units (including departments or programs), courses, or resources involved in RCR education**

    We counted approximately 350 total participants in the Project for Scholarly Integrity events. Our estimate for the breakdown is as follows.

    a. Students: 200
    b. Faculty: 130
    c. Staff: 20
    d. Departments (please list)
        We did not ask participants to identify their program affiliation, but observe that participants represented disciplines in the biological and biomedical sciences, natural sciences, humanities, social sciences and public health sciences.
    e. New resources developed (courses, web resources, print materials, campus programs, etc.)

        o   Through the speaker series event *Animals in Research,* we developed a number of new contacts in the Atlanta veterinary sciences community. Veterinarians who participated in this session received continuing education credit.
        o   We are developing a repository of course resources specific to areas of importance to Emory programs.
        o   In the summer of 2011, we will begin offering train-the-trainer workshops to develop faculty capacity for teaching scholarly integrity.

10. **How has your university made use of the collective assessments (Activities and Climate) adopted by the universities in the Project for Scholarly Integrity?**

    LGS inventoried current RCR/scholarly integrity offerings in the summer and fall of 2009. Results were relayed to CGS in early 2010. The Inventory has helped to guide discussions around possible program models to integrate RCR education into graduate education here at Emory. The Inventory also helped to guide the selection of faculty to include in program modeling discussions. In October 2010, LGS crafted its own, second inventory survey to get a better idea of what specific RCR areas are being covered by courses in Emory's graduate programs. The results are being discussed with the Directors of Graduate Studies and will inform the next round of discussions on program models.

The *Thrush & Martinson* Climate Survey was administered (via Penn State's Survey Research Center) in January 2010. The data were submitted to Emory in May 2010 and analyzed over the summer. At Emory, the total population surveyed was on the small side compared with the larger public research universities in the national project. Our response rate was about 20%. To get more powerful analysis, we combined programs into their divisions (natural science, social science, and humanities). Viewed at this level, there were no clear deficiencies according to the climate survey. We will perform additional analyses to see if greater statistical sophistication yields any practical distinctions.

11. **What material or online resources has your university developed with the use of CGS/ORI award funds (for example, online resources, pedagogical resources, etc.)? Please provide links to online resources below.**

LGS has created a website for the project (and eventual program), which will house information specific to the nine core areas of RCR, pedagogical materials and resources, professional codes of conduct and a page that directs those with questions or concerns to specific persons or groups at Emory who might be able to assist. LGS has begun collecting many of these materials. Once a program model is decided on, LGS will evaluate the use of the website as the primary repository of training, curricular, and pedagogical materials. The site will continue to be developed this year and will likely not be live until a program model is officially adopted. We will continue to assess our time and available resources to build an informational website before any advanced program is adopted more formally. With the goal of a 'required' program that has broad and deep faculty acceptance, commitment and engagement, we will think through the strategic advantage of the website and other media for faculty engagement as we design and implement the larger program.

12. **What learning assessment tools has your university used to assess the efficacy of courses, modules, or other pedagogical resources? Have these tools been used to reflect on the efficacy of project activities? If so, how?**

Not applicable at this time as a program model has not yet been adopted or implemented. However, LGS administration and PIs are consulting with colleagues at other institutions on assessment mechanisms employed in their programs.

13. **Has your university received feedback from campus groups (graduate students, faculty, staff, or other senior administrators) about the project during and following implementation? What have you learned from this feedback?**

As previously discussed, LGS assembled a steering committee to help plan initial programming and to raise campus-wide awareness about the project. The steering committee not only helped to guide programming, particularly for the speaker series, but provided feedback on the inventory and climate assessment templates. They also offered suggestions about the composition of the *Program Working Group* and the structure and focus of the program modeling meetings. The Program Working Group has provided invaluable feedback about the project and is helping LGS to translate that feedback into a program that will be successful and have the ground support, that is, from the faculty and student body, to meet the needs of LGS's diverse constituency. The Program Working Group also represents a helpful range of engaged colleagues who have emerged as leaders in our efforts. LGS is also in discussion with all Directors of Graduate Studies about the project, inviting their attendance at the open forums to get their feedback on the modeling principles and pedagogical goals.

14. **How important to your university's project was its collaborative activities with other awardee and/or affiliate institutions? What kinds of networks with other universities or model resources (i.e. meetings or workshop sessions with other senior university administrators, models or toolkits, online databases of resources, listservs or chat groups, etc.) would be most useful to universities implementing a similar program?**

As part of the CGS site visit, we invited Assistant Dean Doug James from Duke University. Dean James provided a number of insightful comments about the program structures that had been under discussion. He was particularly useful in helping understand how different kinds of programs might be administered. These considerations have been important as we develop our program. In addition, the activities of CGS, especially those tied to annual meetings, have been important for networking, generation of ideas, productive guidance and helpful criticism, and information sharing. The CGS PSI/RCR newsletter continues to be valuable as well.

15. **Will your university sustain the activities that it implemented during the Project for Scholarly Integrity beyond the period of the CGS/ORI award? Please briefly explain any plans or challenges related to the sustainability of your project.**

The Laney Graduate School at Emory University full endorsed the goals of the CGS-ORI initiative and grant funding. We share the CGS-ORI commitment to develop programs in RCR/SI education and we will continue our work to implement comprehensive training across the Laney Graduate School. In this respect, the CGS grant will have a lasting imprint on graduate education at Emory.

One of the challenges is to adopt a plan that is more or less faculty-driven. The plan or model will need to have flexibility and be adaptable to different program and their expanding needs in research ethics. As we move forward, programs will need encouragement to continue to develop appropriate course content.

Another task will be to develop the administrative support necessary to track student participation, recruit faculty, and evaluate program effectiveness. This added administrative structuring will also require additional financial commitments. LGS is committed to establishing sustained resources, in personnel and in finances, as part of our overarching programs for professionalization programs (preparing future faculty and professionals).

Finally, we are continuing to explore best practices for program evaluation. The development of evaluation tools that reflect student abilities to reason about issues in research ethics, rather than test for compliance, is an important, highly valued, and crucial part of sustaining and growing RCR/SI program excellence.

Michigan State University

CGS Project on Scholarly Integrity
Final Report

Karen Klomparens, Principal Investigator
Associate Provost of Graduate Education and Dean, Graduate School

Deans of the graduate schools at Michigan State University (MSU), Pennsylvania State University (PSU), and the University of Wisconsin—Madison (UW-M) are concerned about the influence of questionable research practices and professional acts on the educational opportunities and integrity of their students pursuing advanced degrees and on the quality of research. These influences are short-term through impacts on the graduate experience directly and long-term through how graduates represent their institutions, their professions, and themselves. Ultimately, today's graduate students will be tomorrow's professors; the habits and values they develop will set the climate for the next generation of scholars.

Each university has programs focused on education, instruction, and training in responsible conduct of research (RCR), as well as policies to implement federal requirements. The MSU Graduate School established its RCR program in 1998 (http://grad.msu.edu/rcr/), a research mentoring task force in 2004 (http://grad.msu.edu/publications/docs/integrityresearch.pdf), and a Research Integrity Council in 2007. As graduate school leaders, we recognize our pivotal responsibility in fostering and sustaining environments that promote integrity in research and scholarly pursuits across multiple levels, and for encouraging department and interdisciplinary graduate programs, as well as among individual laboratories and graduate committees, to take local leadership of these initiatives.

Consistent with findings and recommendations from research integrity experts, we adopted a multi-level systems perspective for this project. As a collaborative, we focused on more than just RCR education programs, as we believe education alone will not go far enough in ensuring scholarly integrity. *How People Learn* (NRC, 2000) explicitly focuses on the importance of the learning environment as a critically important part of the system required for effectiveness. A recent published commentary by Melissa Anderson (2007) also suggested a systems approach:

> *... RCR instruction and mentoring are less reliable inhibitors of misbehavior in science than one might assume or hope. Either training in responsible science needs to be improved, or other means need to be found to promote integrity in science. My recommendations address both strategies. First, the responsible conduct of research needs to be communicated through good instructional practices. Second, group mentoring may counter some of the ill effects of individual mentoring seen in our study. Third, preparation for survival in the tough, competitive environment of science should accompany RCR training. Fourth, a shift to collective openness in the research culture offers promise as a way to promote research integrity.*

Because MSU had an active RCR program for more than a decade, we wanted our future efforts to be informed by institutional data. With the NSF requirement for additional education in research integrity beginning half way through this project, our desire for additional assessment of our campus became even more useful. We wanted to know what our graduate programs did well in the area of RCR prior to this project, and with what efforts we might assist them, after an assessment of the current status.

The MSU project consisted of 3 components: a collaborative effort with MSU-PSU-UW-M to refine, administer, analyze, and use an existing RCR climate survey and two additional MSU-specific projects: a content analysis of MSU graduate handbooks for language specific to RCR, research and scholarly integrity and related topics, and the use of the CGS "inventory" of RCR practices and activities across all graduate programs. This later project was conducted by the MSU Research Integrity Council. Since CGS did not develop a separate RCR climate survey, but rather made ours available to the other PSI universities, we did not have a comparison survey to work with, as was originally proposed.

Collaborative project across the 3 universities: the Climate Survey for Responsible Research Practices (as a research project and an intervention)

In August/September 2008, we assembled a team to adapt the existing Uniform Research Integrity Climate Assessment ("U-RICA" =RCR climate) survey (copyright by Carol Thrush; Thrush et al, 2007) to be used for a wide variety of disciplines and audiences at MSU, PSU, and UW-M. The survey team was 2 consultants: Dr. Carol Thrush (U Arkansas Medical Sciences) and Dr. Brian Martinson (HealthPartners, MN); and members of the university collaborative: Dr. Terry May and Dean Karen Klomparens (MSU), Dr. Jim Wells and Dr. Eileen Callahan (UW-M), and Michele Stickler and Dr. Mark Wardell (PSU). With a change in graduate school administration at PSU, Dr. Suzanne Adair and Dr. Vasilatos-Younken took over, with Dean Hank Foley during the final few months.

Drs. Martinson and Thrush are currently completing related research on a revised U-RICA survey with a focus on academic health science center researchers (NIH R21 RR0252729-01) to establish the psychometric properties and refine development of the U-RICA. Content validity of the questions had already been established in past research (Thrush, 2007). From their proposal (with the permission of Drs. Martinson and Thrush):

> *In attempting to promote the integrity of scientific research, most, if not all research organizations would prefer an internal, **self-regulatory** approach over one based on compliance with externally imposed mandates. In addition, responsible faculty strongly prefer a positive approach based on communicating institutional and disciplinary values that are the foundation for excellent research. How well self-regulation works for this purpose, however, and its variability across universities, remain open questions. Appropriate targeting of educational interventions or **organizational change** initiatives to promote research integrity require that organizations have the ability to collect reliable data to benchmark baseline conditions, to assess areas needing improvement, and to subsequently assess the impact of specific initiatives.*

During September 2008-February 2009, MSU convened the survey group to meet in a weekly conference call to discuss each question on the original URICA survey. Since, each university planned to survey ALL graduate programs (beyond just biomedical) and all participants (faculty, postdocs, graduate students, undergraduates, technicians), some survey questions were revised. The survey team convened in Washington DC on December 5 and 6, 2008 for an additional 8 hours of face-to-face discussion to make final decisions on the questions. These more than 100 person-hours of discussion were vital to our revisions of the questions for a wide campus audience of participants.

During March 2009, each university gathered the email addresses for the participants (nearly 30,000 across all 3 institutions). Communication emails were finalized to introduce the survey as "coming up", for the survey itself, and for the reminders. Each University submitted an IRB application once the survey, informed consent, and communications documents were completed. The PSU survey center wrote the code necessary to launch the web-based survey.

The survey was launched in mid-April 2009 and was open for 5 weeks (Survey is on file at CGS). Each university contact person (Stickler at PSU, Wells at UW, and Klomparens at MSU responded to dozens of emails weekly—useful data on concerns, questions, and issues were gathered!). Anecdotally, our MSU Research Integrity Officer reported more information request calls during the 5 weeks that the survey was administered, than he usually receives in a year, demonstrating that a survey is also an intervention.

The core principles used to launch the survey and encourage support focused on our past initiatives at MSU (and similar for PSU and UW-M)**: this is about the quality of research and our responsibilities to our graduate students and postdocs, as well as the public that funds our research.** Because we've used this language consistently over more than a dozen years in the Graduate School, the Vice President for Research, and the Office of the Provost, it was not a surprise to the faculty. Our focus is on the responsible conduct of research and scholarship. For us, this language explicitly focuses on the expectation of "responsibility" to various audiences (students, colleagues, funders) for quality research.

The MSU participation rate was 45% (9916 emails) and was similar across each institution. At MSU: faculty response rate: 54%, graduate students: 43%, undergraduates: 30% with approximately 65% postdocs (who are difficult to define as a population).

Since MSU has espoused the concept of RCR for more than a decade, we did not encounter any obstacles that were not overcome by discussion with faculty. If anything, those not engaged in research for publication, but rather research related to course work assignments (something we in the Graduate School still define as "research") had the most difficult time grappling with what RCR meant to them (outside of FFP as an obvious misconduct problems).

We now know that other universities using the survey have not had the same success with the participation rate. After discussion with our survey team, we pose the following as possible reasons: the Big Ten schools are well- known and respected by each other, as well as cooperating on many programs in graduate education which may have led to a spirit of collaboration (or competition!); the 3 deans have each served for > 10 years in their roles (PSU and UW-M are also VPRs) and are trusted by the faculty; the survey was administered <u>prior</u> to the NSF requirement, perhaps making it more of a research project which faculty respect, rather than a "compliance" project; emails, reminders and other survey tools were well-timed, or there could be other reasons that we have not considered. For us, the collaboration proved to be useful as well as intellectually stimulating. We received feedback from Dr. Thrush and Dr. Martinson that they also found the applied aspects of the survey across 3 institutions with deans' thoughts and concerns to be very helpful to their validation research.

June-August 2009: the survey team again convened by conference call weekly or bi-weekly to clean up the data. Consensus was reached on which questions to drop, the rules (and why) on which participant data to drop, and the process by which the data will be analyzed both collectively and independently by university. Again, these nearly 100—person hours of discussion were important to establish how we would analyze the data, as well as general discussion about what responses might mean for future planning. I make a point of the number of hours of discussion during this project because I believe that too often this type of interaction is greatly under-valued in terms of advancing our collective knowledge on an initiative that many believe is already "finalized".

July 2009: We met with the other universities in the PSI at the CGS summer meeting, to explain use of the survey. Each of the PSI partner universities used the survey during Spring 2010.

Survey Outcomes: Data Analysis, Dashboards, Survey Codebook, Survey User's Manual

(The various "products" resulting from the survey are detailed later in this report). The process we used to arrive at those products follows:

We grouped the survey questions into 8 composite measures in 3 major bins:

Departmental/Program
<u>Expectations</u>—2 questions--e.g., How fair are your department/program's expectations with respect to publishing?

<u>Integrity Norms</u>—11 questions--e.g., How committed are people in your department/program to maintaining data integrity and data confidentiality?

<u>Integrity Socialization</u>—11 questions--e.g., How able are people in your department/program to define research misconduct?

Integrity Inhibitors—11 questions--e.g., How true is it that pressure to produce "positive findings" has a negative effect on the judgment of researchers in your department/program?

Advisor-Advisee Relations– 3 questions--e.g., How fairly do advisors/supervisors treat advisees/supervisees?

Institutional

Institutional Regulatory Quality—4 questions--e.g., How useful are your university's policies/guidelines for the responsible conduct of research?

Institutional RCR Resources—5 questions--e.g., .How effective are the available educational opportunities for learning about responsible research practices (e.g., lectures, seminars, web-based courses, etc.) at your university?

Combined Departmental/Program and Institutional

Global Climate of Integrity—4 questions—e.g., How committed are people in your department/program to maintaining high standards of integrity in their research/scholarship?

MSU college and department summaries across these measures along with "dashboards" and bar graphs (for exquisitely obvious comparisons) were developed (the PPT with examples is on file (and on the web) at CGS –as part of the July 2010 presentation at the Summer Meeting in San Juan, P.R.).

The collaborative agreed to a high standard on which segregate the data into groups to analyze our data: for the scale 1-5 for the survey questions, we chose 4.5. We also chose to provide the average percent for the "no basis for judging" (NBFJ) response. Depending on the question, we used the NBFJ response as a proxy for either little or no knowledge on a particular item or at least that it was not discussed as part of the department or graduate program community interactions.

Each University presented these data in similar ways and to similar audiences in order to continue our systems approach to educating the campus communities in a positive way about the survey results. At MSU, Dean Klomparens presented the collegiate data to the research and graduate associate deans groups. Each were presented only their own college data (which included MSU summary comparison data) Each associate dean also had a quartile ranking sheet for each of the 8 composite factors on which only their programs/departments were listed. **This proved to be the single most useful presentation format for highlighting how individual departments and programs compared to others in the college!** It was obvious at a glance, if a college had programs in each quartile, mostly in the bottom, or mostly in the top. And this comparison helped us avoid the usual ease at ignoring university level data as it is always "some other department or college that brings down the scores, not mine".

College associate deans then shared the individual department/program dashboards and bar graphs with each of the units within their administrative purview. Discussions are still on-going. Members of the Graduate School have been invited to present these data and to engage in discussions with faculty, graduate students, and postdocs on how to improve their climate.

Drs. May and Klomparens also convened a group of postdocs for discussions on RCR climate for them, as some of the most isolated individuals conducting research on any campus, as part of a project funded by the National Postdoc Association http://www.nationalpostdoc.org/programs-resources/past-npa-programs/bring-rcr-home). They attended our MSU Graduate School RCR program and then discussed the topics in relation to their personal experiences.

MSU is continuing to analyze aspects of the data. Our most current application is that of comparing the responses of those whose bachelor's degree was from a non-U.S. institution (as a proxy for international). A few preliminary indications (within the caveats of how individuals interpret specific questions): 46% of international students agreed that their research depends on the work of others, while 65% of domestic students agreed. But that when international and domestic student responses were combined, that in years 0-2, 62% of students agreed that their research depended on the work of others, but at 3+ years, 54% agreed with that statement. For postdocs, the results were more striking: 51% of international postdocs agreed that their research depended on the work of others, while 81% of the domestic postdocs agreed with this statement.

The University of Wisconsin (not submitting their own individual report to CGS), developed summary results for 119 graduate programs at UW-Madison with 4 or more respondents (N = 3,785). The provided comparative results for 8 composite measures (mean, proportion scoring above cut-point, campus percentiles), as well as each programs own and campus-wide item-by-item results. They presented overall results to Graduate School deans and associate deans for research of campus schools/colleges.. They then sent results to 119 graduate programs (directed to departmental chair and graduate program chair) and provided assistance in data interpretation and posted FAQs and RCR resources on the web. Dr. Jim Wells and Dr. Eileen Callahan should be contacted for more specific information on the survey use at UW-Madison.

Survey support materials from the collaborative

For universities wishing to use this survey, CGS has a copy of our <u>Survey Codebook</u> with a technical description of the survey elements and the resulting composite measures. Please note that with the additional revisions expected by Drs. Thrush and Martinson, potential users of the survey may wish to contact them directly for the most recent information.

The consortium produced a <u>User's Manual</u> (on file at CGS) with the following information:

- Background and Survey Development
- Terms of Permission to Use the Survey
- Survey Description
- Survey Administration Considerations
- Scale Creation Notes & Considerations
- SAS Code for Computing the Eight Climate Composite Measures
- List of Demographic Questions & Climate Questions
- List of Composite Measures Descriptions & Items Represented

Drs. Thrush and Martinson expect to release their validated survey into the Creative Commons at the conclusion of their NIH research on the psychometric analysis of the survey (late in 2010).

MSU, PSU, UW-M., Thrush, and Martinson advice to survey users

During our hundreds of person-hours of discussions pre- and post-survey over approximately 16 months, we collectively offer the following advice for universities wishing to use this or any RCR climate survey:

- Define and identify your desired sample populations: who participates in research? Be prepared to address results with each group.
- Obtain lists of emailing addresses well in advance (e.g., HR, directories)
- Have sufficient information on your departmental units to be able to denominate internal units for reporting (#'s invited, #'s responded) {=know your own context}
- <u>Seriously</u> attend to notification and good will communications, these include leadership emails, newsletters (3-6 weeks prior), and a knowledgeable and trusted person (at MSU it was Klomparens) to answer <u>every</u> email question, phone call, or concern during the survey

- Map out survey process, including the mode of delivery and return (web or paper) (IT assistance if you need it!),
- Plan the timing of implementation for your academic calendar, and the timing and number of reminders
- Keep the VPR and Provost informed

Our suggested guidelines for using your data effectively:

- Identify 1 or 2 composite measures or even single survey items as the focus for your campus or for particular graduate programs or departments
- Present the "dashboard" data in context with other similar units on campus
- Link to the NSF RCR requirement and ongoing improvement efforts for quality research, not just compliance
- Offer support, resources, and guidance from the Graduate School
- Make results as public as possible to encourage serious attention to the issues, but not to "beat up" departments
- Volunteer to work with individual units as they strive to improve their climate

We continue the analysis of our survey data and engage in discussions with faculty and administrators. Since RCR education has been sustained as a focus at MSU for more than a decade, the PSI initiative will be folded into that focus. **The data from the survey was immeasurably useful as we could provide tangible data with a very good response rate to help faculty understand the current climate in their own graduate programs.**

MSU additional projects

Dr. Stephanie Watts (Pharmacology/Toxicology) and Dr. Gail Dummer (Kinesiology), Dr. James Pivarnik (RIO and Kinesiology) participated in this part of the project, along with Dr. May, Research Assistant, Parker Huston, and Dean Klomparens.

As a result of the survey results, we revised our learning objectives for the Graduate School sponsored RCR program.

MSU's Research Integrity Council (RIC), chaired by Dr. Watts, completed a project of

RCR/Scholarly integrity posters (http://grad.msu.edu/ric/), a set of which were sent to each of our 120 graduate programs for posting in their buildings and labs. These follow the guidelines developed in 2003-04 by a committee chaired by an MSU member of the National Academy of Sciences, the late Dr. Hans Kende (http://grad.msu.edu/researchintegrity/docs/ris04.pdf). These posters represent the areas of RCR defined by ORI, but do so in broader language that our focus-groups determined would better capture the attention of our faculty and graduate students.

The RIC administered the CGS "inventory" of RCR-related activities and analyzed the results. Research Integrity Council prepared a "Needs Statement" for affirmative education in responsible conduct in research and creative activities as a result of their analysis of the inventories. That statement was presented to the Vice President for Research and Graduate Studies, Dr. Ian Gray. Dr. Watts and Dr. Gray are working on an implementation timeline for the most pressing issues in the Needs Assessment.

The inventories proved to be very helpful as the RIC moved forward with its initiative for RCR next steps at MSU. The inventories (and the survey data) were also used as each graduate program designed an educational program to meet the NSF requirement.

We continue to work with our English Language Center, Office for International Students and Scholars, and Ombudsman to develop more effective learning tools for our international graduate students and postdocs, especially on the issue of plagiarism.

Graduate Handbook Content Analysis

Our objective was to tie the climate survey data to the ongoing efforts of the RIC (see above) with an analysis of graduate handbooks; handbooks that represent the explicit expectations of a program faculty for its graduate students academic and professional development. Assuring that we inform and educate all scholars about these matters is a realistic and important goal for our university RCR efforts.

We performed content analysis on the graduate handbooks for our 11 partner department/programs (Biochemistry and Molecular Biology, interdisciplinary program in Cell and Molecular Biology, Interdisciplinary program in Genetics, Interdisciplinary program in Integrative Environmental Toxicology, Microbiology and Molecular Genetics, Interdisciplinary program in Neuroscience, Nursing Ph.D., Pharmacology and Toxicology, Physiology, and Psychology) looking words or statements on RCR and the importance of scholarly integrity and for explicit language that incorporates the concepts, expectations, and ideas of scholarly integrity into the specifics of the graduate program and its disciplinary context.

Each Handbook had the statements required by MSU's University Graduate Council 5 years ago http://grad.msu.edu/publications/docs/studentadvising.pdf and http://grad.msu.edu/publications/docs/integrityresearch.pdf, as well as the expected additional statements regarding specific areas of RCR required in the discipline (e.g., protection of human subjects, humane use of animals, misconduct, data management). We found no obvious correlation between the frequency or kind of statements about RCR and the outcomes of the survey related to the placement of each of the units on the quartile summary sheets for the 8 composite measures of the climate survey.

This was the least useful of our PSI activities at MSU. What is said or written, is not always embedded in the culture, even though it may be a useful first step. As an additional example of this, at our September 14, 2010 seminar on RCR, using the personal response system, students were asked if they had a copy of their handbook; 105 of 131 said yes. They were asked if they had read through the handbook, even briefly, only 14 said yes, although a few indicated that faculty specifically pointed out the handbook statements about research integrity.

Connection of PSI to the current NSF requirement for RCR education

We are linking our PSI project initiatives to the current NSF requirement for RCR education. In fact, MSU is requiring formal education and training for all graduate students, postdocs, and undergraduates engaged in research, regardless of funding source (or no funding source). http://www.grad.msu.edu/ric/docs/WilcoxMemo.pdf

With the results of the survey and inventory in hand, and linking to the newly established NSF requirement for RCR education and training, MSU colleges and departments began to develop their own, disciplinary-specific RCR programs using the resources (powerpoints, videos, case studies) collected and developed by the Graduate School http://grad.msu.edu/researchintegrity/. Each college/department has an individualized plan for its graduate students and postdocs. Most plans are being implemented this Fall semester 2010.

Common core areas for these programs include: avoiding plagiarism, research misconduct, conflict of interest policies, ethical decision-making, and mentor-mentee relationship (using our task force reports mentioned earlier). Also required as core components, but to be delivered individually by faculty with his/her own students: peer review, authorship, data management, access and control, and collaborative research. For those areas in which it is appropriate, human research protection and/or the humane treatment of animals are also included.

The Graduate School RCR program effectively uses a response system in our seminars as part of the assessment of learning. For an audience of 150-200 across multiple disciplines, this permits us to gather data on the areas of most concern or lack of understanding by students to better inform our choice of content and to assess learning, provides the presenter with instant data on which to base further discussions, and provides the students with feedback on their peers' knowledge and concerns. In addition, one important advantage of a central seminar is being able to bring in the Research Integrity Officer, the VP for Research, and the IRB staff, to talk directly to the students (we are also capturing these lessons in videos for our students conducting research around the globe). These individuals would not have the time to meet with 14 colleges or more than 100 individual programs, yet they represent very credible sources of information and want to be approachable by any member of the research community with questions.

For the college and department programs, some education is on-line, other is required to be face-to-face. The "curriculum" is lodged in our AN-GEL course management system and includes the resources mentioned above. In addition, we are working on embedded quizzes (with answers and explanations) as well as pre-tests. These will help us determine the learning that has taken place from the various curricular approaches to RCR. It may not, however, determine the subsequent behavior or culture, although we hope the learning is related (Heitman and Anastidu, 2005). MSU instituted a non-credit registration system to track graduate student, postdocs, technicians, and undergraduates and their completion of these RCR modules.

References

Anderson, M. S. 2007. Collective Openness and Other Recommendations for the Promotion of Research Integrity. Science and Engineering Ethics 13:387-394.

Bransford, J. D., Brown, A. L., and Cocking, R. R., (Editors) 2000. *How People Learn*. National Academies Press, Washington, DC pp. 153, 190.

Heitman, E., L. Anestidou, et al. (2005). "Do researchers learn to overlook misbehavior?" Hastings Cent Rep 35(5): 49.

Institute of Medicine and National Research Council Committee on Assessing Integrity in Research Environments. *Integrity in Scientific Research: Creating an Environment that Promotes Responsible Conduct.* Washington, D.C.: The National Academies Press; 2002.

Thrush C.R., Vander Putten, J., Rapp, C.G., Pearson, L.C., Berry, K.S., O'Sullivan, P.S. Content validation of the Organizational Climate for Research Integrity (OCRI) survey. *Journal of Empirical Research on Human Research Ethics.* December 2007; 2 (4):35-52.

Penn State University

CGS Project for Scholarly Integrity
Final Report

Henry Foley, Principal Investigator
Vice President for Research, Dean of the Graduate School
Suzanne Adair, Co-PI
Assistant Dean of the Graduate School

Presentation of RCR Initiatives

Penn State began discussions about implementing our overall Scholarly Integrity Initiative during the 2008-2009 academic year. This initiative, which later became known as the Scholarship and Research Integrity program (SARI), was introduced in the fall of 2009. The initiative was introduced as a way to promote the responsible conduct of research within the university community and to educate faculty, staff and students about the importance of research integrity as outlined in the Council of Graduate Schools' report *Graduate Education for the Responsible Conduct of Research*. The SARI initiative includes program specific and interdisciplinary components to ensure that topics related to RCR are comprehensively addressed, using two specific mechanisms. First, all incoming graduate students are required to complete the Collaborative Institutional Training Initiative (CITI) training during their first year in their programs. Secondly, students must then complete an additional five hours of discussion based RCR training before completing their programs. Each academic college was tasked with developing their own five hour discussion based education component to ensure that it addressed particular issues related to specific disciplines. Each college submitted their plans to our Office of Research Protections (ORP) for final approval.

In the midst of the SARI initiative, Penn State joined Michigan State and the University of Wisconsin, along with several other schools in the Project for Scholarly Integrity (PSI). Although Penn State's SARI program had not been officially rolled out when the PSI began in the spring of 2009, there had been hours of discussion and planning across the colleges to prepare for program implementation of the SARI so the community was very aware of the university's plan to promote education and training on RCR issues. Given this, it is difficult to separate the PSI from the university's own SARI program in terms of community recognition. During the beginning stages of the PSI, faculty, postdocs, research associates and graduate students at Penn State, Michigan State and Wisconsin were asked to complete the U-RICA Climate Survey and the academic programs were asked to submit Activities Assessments in an effort to determine the climate of research integrity across the university. At Penn State, it wasn't until the results of the U-RICA survey were fully reviewed with administrators across the university that some in the community became more aware of the difference between the two initiatives.

We experienced some challenges with the implementation of the PSI as a result of administrative changes at Penn State as all three of the administrators responsible for the project left the university. This transition impacted the course of the project as new administrators were assigned to the initiative and brought up to speed. Subsequently, some components of this project were not implemented precisely at the time they were originally scheduled to be conducted which limited the amount of communication about it to the larger university community. For this reason, we would recommend to other institutions that they have secondary personnel assigned to a project such as this who are prepared to provide backup for project leaders. Having additional staff involved would help with maintaining program continuity, allowing for continuous communication and progress with no break in activity if there is any loss of personnel.

Program Implementation

In April 2009, the PSI was launched as the U-RICA Survey was conducted across the university. 12,300 emails were sent out to faculty, postdocs, research associates and graduate students. There were 5600 respondents, which gave Penn State about a 45.5% response rate. As noted above, during the same period, each academic program was asked to complete an Activities Assessment, which would identify the various ways that they provide RCR education to their students and how their students are informed about such initiatives. These two activities were duplicated at each of the institutions involved in the project.

Each institution conducted additional activities to further support the goals of the PSI. At Penn State, we chose to pilot an RCR educational training initiative using faculty members as trainers. We conducted RCR training sessions for faculty members who would serve as facilitators for RCR workshops conducted for graduate students within the College of Health and Human Development. The faculty trainings were led by staff from the ORP during the spring of 2009. The student sessions, which occurred during the 2009–10 academic year, consisted of two evening workshops for each series, which lasted for two hours each. Students were given a pre and post assessment to evaluate their overall learning.

In the spring of 2010, the U-RICA Survey results were disseminated to the Associate Deans of each college who followed up by initiating discussions about the results with the programs within their colleges. Survey results for Penn State were quite positive with overall scores on the eight factors ranging from a low of 3.47 on the *Institutional Integrity Resources* factor to a high of 4.24 on the *Global Climate of Integrity* factor. It is of particular interest to note that one academic college scored the highest on seven of the eight factors. Several factors were identified as target areas in general as they received somewhat lower scores: *Institutional Integrity Resources, Program Integrity Socialization, Program Integrity Inhibitors, and Program Advisor-Advisee Relationships.*

The college level conversations are designed to assist programs with developing additional strategies to address any RCR areas that need to be strengthened such as the four areas noted above. These discussions will be followed up with a second iteration of the U-RICA Survey in an effort to determine whether there has been any change in the climate of research integrity after these initiatives.

The workshops, online training and college level discussions include a focus on all 9 core areas of Responsible Conduct for Research: Data Acquisition, Management, Sharing, and Ownership; Conflicts of Interest and Commitment; Human Subjects; Animal Welfare; Research Misconduct; Publication Practices and Responsible Authorship; Mentor and Trainee Responsibilities; Peer Review; and Collaborative Research.

One of the RCR initiatives that proved to be most successful was providing training for faculty members who volunteered to facilitate RCR workshops with graduate students. Although the training was initially offered to faculty members from HHD, those from other colleges requested to participate. Additionally, while there has been some discussion about the likelihood that junior faculty members are more likely to participate in conversations about RCR topics, many of the HHD faculty members who requested to be trained were senior faculty members.

Despite the success of training faculty members to facilitate RCR workshops with graduate students, during conversations across campus, there was full agreement that we need to increase faculty participation in all aspects of RCR education. Involving faculty members in this type of initiative more fully was viewed as the most important component of a successful RCR educational initiative and that attention to this particular aspect is critical.

While all of our incoming graduate students are required to participate in RCR education through the online CITI training and the college level discussion based requirements, it is difficult to know how many students overall have been involved with other RCR activities within the colleges. Many students and postdocs participate in brown bag sessions and other professional development sessions on RCR topics provided by ORP throughout the year and academic programs across the university provide opportunities for learning through orientations and courses. Given the requirements of the SARI program, we know that at some point within the next several years every graduate student will have participated in RCR educational activities.

Utilization of Instruments, Resources and Assessments

We have utilized the U-RICA Climate Survey in the same manner as other institutions within the project. Survey results were disseminated to and discussed with the Associate Deans who were tasked with disseminating results to their programs and to facilitate follow up discussions about how to address areas that may need attention. To date, we have not utilized the results of the Activities Assessments but will do so shortly. We are also very interested in learning the results from the CGS analysis of these Activities Assessments.

We have not developed any new material or online resources with these funds and currently utilize existing resources within the university to promote RCR concepts and educate students, faculty and staff on all areas related to research integrity.

We have conducted pre and post workshop assessments with graduate students in the College of Health and Human Development who participated in the RCR workshops facilitated by faculty members, but have not completed an analysis of that data at this point.

Reflections and Sustainability

As noted earlier, the most significant challenge we faced was experiencing a complete turnover of project staff after the departure of all three members of the PSU team halfway through the project. Given such turnover, the challenges were reassigning project tasks, ensuring that the new team was sufficiently able to get acclimated to the project and to the larger PSI team from other institutions, and to regenerate interest within the PSU community. It was especially beneficial to have the new project coordinator participate in conference calls and regularly scheduled meetings with those from other schools and

CGS soon after the transition. These contacts provided an opportunity for the new project leader to ask questions about the history of the project and to get a better perspective of how Penn State's initiatives were both similar to and different from RCR practices at other institutions.

One of our recommendations for any institution considering the implementation of this type of project would be to ensure that the project team consisted of several faculty members, as well as representatives from the Office of Research Protections and the Dean's office. Including current faculty members would ensure that any categorization of academic programs for assessments regarding RCR climate and activities is done correctly. This would also ensure that faculty members were present during conversations about involving faculty in general in RCR education initiatives. Throughout discussions about the project, including during the CGS visit, we consistently heard that it was necessary to engage in conversations about RCR at multiple levels and to begin the dialogue with junior faculty in an effort to create the greatest impact on the research climate across the university. Additionally, allowing academic colleges to develop RCR programs that are specifically designed to address the issues within their disciplines was viewed as a critical component of implementing a successful university wide RCR initiative. All of these aspects are viewed as important steps to ensuring that future generations of researchers will be prepared to conduct research.

Penn State has a long history of providing RCR education and is fully committed to continuing to do so. As noted, RCR education is primarily the responsibility of the ORP who will continue to develop initiatives which promote scholarly integrity among faculty, staff and students. The variety of activities that are provided by ORP, which include workshops and trainings, individual consultations, online and video resources and quarterly newsletters have been widely utilized and requested, which demonstrates the community's commitment to conducting research in a manner that is both thorough and ethical. And as new issues in research emerge, we are certain that the university will develop effective mechanisms to address those as well.

University of Alabama at Birmingham

CGS Project for Scholar Integrity
Final Report

Bryan D. Noe, Principal Investigator
Dean, Graduate School
Jeffrey Engler, Co-PI
Associate Dean for Academic Affairs, UAB Graduate School

Overview: UAB has offered a graduate course in Research Integrity (GRD 717) since 1992. It was instituted by then Graduate Dean Terry Hickey to meet the NIH requirement that all students supported on T32 training grants receive instruction on ethical conduct of scholarly activity (SI. This course was developed by Dr. Harold Kincaid of the Department of Philosophy at UAB and covers all of the areas of responsible conduct recommended by ORI. Because faculty realized the need for this sort of instruction, this course became a requirement for all graduate students in biomedical science graduate programs, many of whom would have an opportunity to be supported on a training grant at some point in their career. Currently, approximately 120 graduate students take the GRD 717 or equivalent course each year. With the arrival of Dean Bryan Noe, these efforts to expand discussion of scholarly integrity evolved further by the addition of campus-wide workshops, teacher training courses, and ethics education.

1. **How did your university define and communicate the principles of scholarly integrity to the graduate student and faculty community?**

The award of the PSI contract to UAB in 2008 provided an opportunity to re-engage in discussions with students and faculty about the role of ethics education and scholarly integrity in graduate training. Because of the groundwork laid by the GRD 717 course and earlier funding from an NSF/CGS grant, the principles of RCR are familiar to most graduate students.

What we sought to accomplish with the current contract was to move beyond the "one course and I'm done" approach towards ethics education to an approach that embeds SI education into the curriculum. While there were anecdotal reports that students engaged in discussions of scholarly integrity issues while taking a specific course like GRD 717, we wanted to extend further the opportunities for these debates. This change in focus was intended to engage students throughout their graduate training and allow them to revisit topics later in their career progression when they had had a chance to confront these issues during their research.

2. **Activities and interventions—Successes**

Our long term goal is to identify "faculty champions" who will commit to training graduate students in issues of scholarly integrity. To accomplish this goal, we've evaluated strategies for supporting faculty willing to take on this role, by testing various models and resources for developing activities to teach lessons in scholarly integrity We've extensively tested three different approaches for embedding integrity education and providing support for faculty.

a. Workshops, using our "Ethical Authorship/Avoiding Plagiarism" materials. This activity was provided to faculty and to graduate program directors as a free service. It has become a yearly "orientation" activity in several departments. Over the last three years, this workshop has been presented to 24 different student groups (a total of more than 800 students), mainly graduate students. It offered an opportunity to test various strategies for the most effective engagement of the students in thinking about this scholarly problem. The workshop was also adapted for use with faculty and was presented to four faculty groups (three "Excellence in Teaching" seminars for new faculty and one "Freshman Year Experience" faculty seminar); the goal of these faculty seminars was to prepare faculty to provide mentored support for their students as they refined their ethical writing skills.

b. The "Train the Trainer" model for teaching scholarly integrity (Fall semester, 2009 and 2010): The UAB Graduate School offers a course (GRD 715) in training and pedagogy for beginning graduate students who serve as teaching assistants in undergraduate courses in Biology, Chemistry, Physics, Mathematics, and Computer Science. These TAs teach undergraduate students in majors prerequisite to careers in biomedical and behavioral sciences who all take introductory courses in these disciplines. We have used GRD 715 as a laboratory to train these TAs in issues of data integrity by integrating a group assignment in which students develop lesson plans on data integrity for a one-hour presentation to their classes. This assignment allows the TAs to hone their teaching skills while enhancing their understanding of an important ethical issue. Our goal is to test training methods and materials to engage students in discussions of SI as well as to train future faculty members in the importance of ethics education.

c. Testing ethics education materials to support faculty "champions": In collaboration with Drs. Harold Kincaid and Sara Vollmer in the UAB Department of Philosophy, we've created a series of videos to dramatize issues in scholarly integrity ("Amanda's Dilemma" on plagiarism and "Whistleblower" on research misconduct). For these videos, we tested an online approach called "Query—Video—Query" (QVQ) to engage students in reflective thinking in an online setting. More recently, we were impressed by research reported by Dr. Elizabeth Holmes on creating videos in a "decision tree" format, where the viewer can select options at various points of the video and see how that choice affects the eventual outcome.

With funds from this contract, we are creating three videos, two of which have been designed so that we can test the effectiveness of the QVQ and the "decision tree" online presentation approaches for student learning.

3. What were the most successful activities?

a. *"Ethical Authorship/Avoiding Plagiarism" workshops:*
Based on faculty requests, these workshops have been the most popular and the most public of the events that have been sponsored by the CGS/ORI contract, with more than 800 graduate students contacted. Many of these students were in their first or second year of graduate study. These workshops have provided a laboratory in which to test ideas and strategies for effective delivery of content on a specific aspect of scholarly integrity. Types of content developed by our Professional Development staff (Dr. Julia Austin and Jennifer Greer) and tested in the workshop included:

1. Use of video materials—in early workshops, we used the "Amanda's Dilemma" video to start the conversation. Based on subsequent assessments, we learned that the students in the early years of their training did not relate well to the scenario posed by the video—plagiarism of a dissertation. The student audience saw the video as addressing dissertation writing, not plagiarism.

2. Self quiz—We have adapted with a self-quiz on plagiarism that was developed by the Library and Learning Resource Center, Empire State College, State University of New York. It poses five scenarios and asks students to decide whether or not plagiarism is involved. After a few minutes, we discuss the questions and provide the correct answers. This exercise activates student's background knowledge about plagiarism and provides an initial exposure to the "gray areas" of the subject.

3. PowerPoint—"Plagiarism in Academia"—an interactive presentation tests student's ability to assess ethical paraphrase versus "mosaic" plagiarism. This exercise informs them about the consequences to research careers if one plagiarizes and shows that Turnitin is not a foolproof plagiarism detection tool.

4. Case studies—"Developing Ethical GPS". This presentation discusses moral leadership based on the research of Dr. James Rest, using two case studies which prompt students to discuss the nuances and temptations of plagiarism.

5. Critical thinking—"Why we cite". A list of five reasons suggested for why we cite sources in scholarly works. Small groups discuss and rank the 5 reasons, in order of perceived importance.

6. Practice writing—"Ethical Summary Protocol". This presentation challenges students to read a short passage and write a short paraphrase of it, to model good note taking (and plagiarism avoiding) strategies. This exercise shows students that each student's paraphrase of the same material is often very different, despite the brevity of the original passage, thus addressing the oft-heard student complaint that "there's only one way to write this."

7. Presentation—"Binge writing". This short discussion talks about good note-taking, "writing to learn", and cryptomnesia (unconscious recollection of previous materials).

8. Brochure—"The Ethics of Paraphrase". We developed a brochure to summarize the content of the workshop and to provide a quick reference guide to which students can refer: http://www.uab.edu/graduate/publications/plagiarism.pdf.

What we have learned from the "Ethical Authorship" workshop:

1. We found that many graduate students lack confidence in their ability to paraphrase and to assess their own writing for plagiarism. We surveyed more than 500 graduate students who participated in

one of the "Avoiding Plagiarism" workshops. They were asked to rate their confidence (on a scale of 1 (little confidence) to 5 (highly confident)) to perform a number of writing tasks associated with effective academic writing. Participant responses also showed that more than three-fourths of the students thought that plagiarism was a major problem.

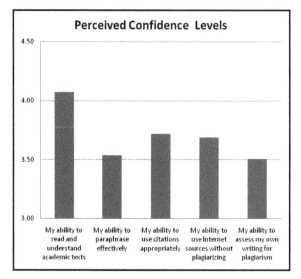

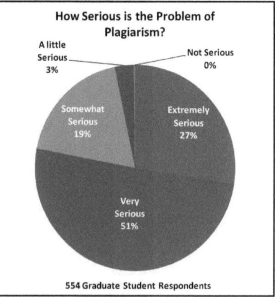

2. We learned to develop many interactive short duration activities (brief lecture, small group, writing and paraphrasing exercises, self-graded quizzes) that could be assembled into workshops targeted at specific graduate student audiences. As we roll these materials out to potential faculty champions, we want to emphasize the "mix and match" nature of these activities, so different components can be assembled to match the needs of the target audience and the learning objective.

3. We needed effective marketing to engage students. To call the workshop "Avoiding Plagiarism" deterred some students. We rebranded it as "Ethical Authorship: Joining the Scholarly Conversation" and emphasized effective and efficient writing strategies that would result in a lower likelihood of plagiarism, but also increased professional integrity and productivity. That changed the student perception of the activities from punitive ("Here's what will happen to you if you plagiarize.") to proactive ("Here's how I will improve my writing and note-taking skills, so I don't have to worry about plagiarism.")

b. *Embedding ethics education in training of teaching assistants*
To be effective at engaging faculty in embedding ethics training into the curriculum, we needed to develop materials to support faculty and to test different strategies for delivering the message. As we have done with the "Avoiding Plagiarism" workshops, we wanted to model strategies and develop effective tools to encourage faculty to use these materials in their courses, journal clubs, and lab meetings. We already train a number of graduate students each Fall semester in how to be effective as teaching assistants for undergraduate courses in the natural sciences and mathematics (GRD 715, taught by Dr. Julia Austin and Nancy Abney of the Graduate School's Professional Development staff). We have used this course as a laboratory to provide TAs with the pedagogic skills necessary to design, test, and deliver a one-hour lesson on academic integrity to their students. Because of the audience of undergraduate students with whom these TAs interact, we chose "data integrity" as the ethics topic for this teaching exercise.

Strategy: The GRD 715 course is a blended course with both face-to-face meetings and online activities.

At the first class meeting, students were provided background reading material and case studies on data integrity, as well as a model of lesson design that incorporated active learning, diversity, and how to develop and assess measurable learning outcomes. A rubric was developed to guide students in the development of their lesson plan on data integrity.

At the second in class meeting, we reviewed the project and assembled groups of three or four TAs into discipline-specific groups (Biology; Chemistry; Physics, Computer and Information Science). Each small group spent 90 minutes in initial discussion of approaches that they believed would be effective for conveying information about data integrity.

Over the next four weeks, each group prepared an outline of a 60 minute lesson plan on data integrity; during the month, they worked on an iterative process of review and revision, first posting rough outlines, getting feedback and suggestions from other groups, revising their lesson plans, and finally meeting face-to-face for a peer critique of the lesson plan.

At the next class meeting, the students were rearranged into groups to further critique the draft plan, using the rubric provided. After 60-75 minutes, the original teaching groups reassembled to discuss the feedback that they received.

Over the next three weeks, the groups rewrote their lesson plans and received more critique and advice from the course instructors.

At the last class meeting, students in each group presented a 15-20 minute presentation describing their lesson plan, for further critique and refinement.

What we learned from training TAs to create lesson plans on data integrity:

1. Students took this project very seriously, developing a creative mixture of materials for use, including short PowerPoint presentations, simulations, case studies, classroom quizzes, brochures, group discussions, peer teaching and short lab experiments.
2. Students appreciated the opportunity to apply what they had learned about pedagogy to developing an actual lesson plan. They drew on relevant current events and incorporated a variety of techniques to engage their students in thoughtful learning.

Future plans:

1. We're working with instructors in undergraduate laboratory classes to provide opportunities to test the lesson plans for their effectiveness with undergraduate student audiences. Our goal is to include one hour discussions of data integrity in the course syllabus of all undergraduate laboratory classes, using the materials prepared by the TAs in GRD 715.
2. We want to collect the materials prepared by the graduate students into short duration components that faculty could use to assemble their own presentations on data integrity. At the end of this semester, we should have four to six different one hour lesson plans that were developed by the TAs in GRD 715.

c. Online videos to engage students in discussion of scholarly integrity

With previous CGS funding, we created two successful videos, "Amanda's Dilemma" and "Whistleblower", for online education of graduate students in issues of plagiarism and whistleblowing (http://www.uab.edu/graduate/rcr/index.html). For these presentations, Dr. Sara Vollmer developed the "Query-Video-Query" approach, in which students are asked an initial question, shown a segment of the video addressing the question, and then asked to reflect on what they have seen. Dr. Nancy Matchett of the University of Northern Colorado prepared the QVQ questions and answers.

Dr. Vollmer learned of the work of Dr. Elizabeth Holmes at the Stockdale Center at the US Naval Academy. Dr. Holmes' approach was to create "decision trees" where an online viewer could choose what path to take at key points in the narrative and observe the consequences of that action. We decided to test which approach (QVQ or decision tree) was the most effective for presentation and reflection on ethics issues.

Because of the protracted nature of video production, we are only now completing the videos. We created two video scripts to test these two different approaches to using video vignettes for online education. The first script, "That's My Paper!", deals with misappropriation of data and the ethical responsibilities that coauthors share. It's based on a real experience of a faculty member at UAB and has been vetted and edited by several senior UAB faculty with substantial academic publishing experience. The second script, "Invention", deals with intellectual property rights of graduate students who participate in research. It was written and edited with substantial input from the UAB Research Foundation, the entity that manages the intellectual property held by UAB. Our videographer, Jana Harris, is currently editing the videos for incorporation into websites.

We're currently filming a third video script, "Cultural Miscommunication", which deals with cultural misunderstandings and data integrity.

4. **What were some of the least successful activities?**

   a. Instituting a graduate student pledge: We worked with the officers of the Graduate Student Association to institute a "graduate student pledge" similar to the one used at the University of Toronto. While the officers were supportive, implementing the pledge itself was difficult, due to other priorities established by the GSA.
   b. Identifying faculty champions: We've had a lot of support from department chairs with regard to the activities of the project. We have also had frequent requests from faculty and campus leaders to present workshops to their students. However, identifying specific faculty champions has been difficult. Many faculty feel substantial stress from the increasingly competitive process to secure research funding; they are often reluctant to commit time to these other duties often regarded as tangential or lower priority.

5. **What were the biggest overall obstacles or challenges?**
   Our biggest challenge was the tension between educational activities and compliance activities within the research community at UAB. The Graduate School has always viewed our role as educational: "What are the potential ethical conflicts and why is it important to resolve them in an appropriate way?" The partnerships that we have formed as part of the PSI have emphasized educational opportunities. We've tried to maintain the distinction that our activities are educational, not compliance. Staff members within the research community who have responsibility for overseeing compliance have expressed the concern that we're not teaching students about how to comply with regulations. We've chosen to focus on "Here's why compliance is important", rather than "Here's how to comply".

6. **Topics that were covered in the activities: Although we covered many of the core areas of RCR education as part of our PSI activities, we focused most intensively on the following areas:**

    a. **Research misconduct (falsification, fabrication, and plagiarism)**—the "Ethical Authorship" Workshops

    b. **Authorship**—the video "That's My Paper!"

    c. **Data acquisition, sharing, ownership, and management**—development of lesson plans for data integrity by the teaching assistants in the GRD 715 course.

    d. **Collaborative scholarship**—the video "Invention"

    e. **Mentor mentee responsibilities**—participated in a university-wide project to identify and publicize best practices for mentoring graduate students, postdoctoral fellows, and junior faculty.

    f. **Publication practices and responsible authorship**—the video "That's My Paper!"

7. **Pedagogical methods tested**

    a. "Ethical Authorship" workshops: short PowerPoint presentations, self-quizzes, student writing exercises, small group discussion, short case studies, text analysis, critical thinking exercises, student evaluations of workshops

    b. Develop pedagogical skills in TA training course (GRD 715): students created a variety of materials, including case studies, brochures, self-tests, role playing, simulations, short demonstrations, small group discussion, short PowerPoint presentations, peer teaching

    c. Video development for online distribution: Our video projects, "That's My Paper!" and "Invention", were developed to be presented online in both the "Query-Video-Query" format and the "Decision Tree" format. In future months, we want to test the effectiveness of each strategy for student learning.

8. **What recommendations do you have for other institutions?**

    a. Form partnerships to develop materials and to engender support: graduate students, faculty, department chairs, deans, officials charged with supporting the research mission of the institution. Use faculty and students to develop and test proposed activities.

b. Use focus groups and surveys to identify those aspects of scholarly integrity where faculty and student perceive the greatest "threat". We used survey results to identify mentorship issues as key concerns of both faculty and students. These issues included authorship, plagiarism, data management, and trust.

9. **Participant numbers**

Students:

"Ethical Authorship" workshops: greater than 700 graduate students and approximately 75 undergraduates. We have evaluations from approximately 75% of those graduate students

TA training in GRD 715—Approximately 45 students over 2 years.

Faculty: Approximately 40 Nursing faculty; approximately 15 faculty in the School of Engineering; 90 faculty in the Excellence in Teaching seminars; approximately 30 faculty in the Freshman Year Experience seminar; various faculty with whom we consulted about content of the activities of the PSI project

Departments and Schools impacted:

School of Nursing; School of Medicine (Biochemistry and Molecular Genetics, Cell Biology, Microbiology, Neurobiology, Physiology and Biophysics, Pathology, Vision Science); Biomedical Engineering; School of Public Health

10. **How have you used the Climate and Activities Assessments?**
Prior to the start of the PSI, we completed a three campus climate survey, including faculty and graduate students from the UAB, UA, and UAH campuses. That survey had an approximately 30% response rate and showed that both faculty and students were concerned about issues of mentoring, authorship, data management, and intellectual honesty. We are still analyzing the data from the climate survey done as part of the PSI. We've had difficulty understanding the ways in which the Penn State Statistics Center did this analysis for the other awardees. In hindsight, we probably should also have used this center to administer the survey and analyze the results.

The Activities assessment has provided us with information about what graduate programs perceive are the ways in which they communicate values and educate students and postdoctoral fellows in scholarly integrity. We intend to follow up with them in a year or two to see if these activities have changed.

11. **Materials Produced**
3 videos ("That's My Paper!", "Invention", "Cultural Miscommunication") for testing as online and in class teaching materials.

PowerPoint teaching materials:

"Plagiarism in America"—a short overview of examples of plagiarism and its effect on students and faculty careers.

"The Rest Analysis"—developing ethical sensitivity in writing—short case studies in authorship/plagiarism for small group discussion

"Why We Cite"—small group discussion presentation for engaging students in good citation practices, to model professional behavior in academic writing

"Ethical Summary Protocol"—practicing how to summarize source materials for good academic writing and avoiding plagiarism.

"Binge Writing"—an interactive presentation/discussion on cryptomnesia (in which previously read writing is unconsciously remembered while writing).

Case studies: "Ethical Authorship" workshops; GRD 715
Self-quizzes: "Ethical Authorship" workshops; GRD 715
Brochures:

"Ethics of Paraphrase"—summary of the "Avoiding Plagiarism workshop information. www.uab.edu/graduate/publications/plagiarism.pdf.

Brochures prepared on data integrity by GRD 715 teaching assistants

12. **Learning assessment tools developed**
    With the "Ethical Authorship" workshops, we have surveyed more than 550 graduate students about their knowledge and experiences with educational materials related to plagiarism and academic writing.

13. **How did you receive feedback from on-campus groups?**
    We received feedback through several channels:

    a. Discussions with research leaders: Dean Noe informed the other deans, the provost, and the Vice President for Research about activities related to the PSI. Associate Dean Engler informed the Council for Translational Research and the Center for Clinical and Translational Science membership about PSI activities. Dr. Engler also represented the PSI project activities in a CCTS-sponsored campus-wide project to highlight best practices in mentoring for students and junior faculty.
    b. Discussions with graduate students: Associate Dean Engler made presentations about PSI activities to the Graduate Student Association. We also meet once per month with the officers of the Graduate Student Association and activities related to the PSI were often discussed.
    c. Discussions with course directors: Because we asked teaching assistants in the GRD 715 course to prepare lesson plans on scholarly integrity (data integrity) for presentation in undergraduate courses, we worked with undergraduate science course directors to find opportunities to test the lesson plans with undergraduate students. This activity will be ongoing, beyond the end of the PSI funding.

14. **How important were the collaborative activities with other PSI awardees or affiliates?**
    The periodic meetings helped us develop our own activities because we could see what best practices had been effective at other institutions. Some of these activities could be adapted to the UAB context. The exchanges between the awardee institutions have also provided a model for graduate deans in Alabama to work together to share resources for promoting scholarly integrity.

15. **How will you sustain the activities implemented during the PSI?**
    UAB has made a continuing commitment to support scholarly integrity throughout the campus. Programs like the PSI allow us to test ideas and provide new supporting materials for furthering that institutional goal. We

intend to seek further opportunities for building and distributing these supporting materials and to identify faculty champions within our campus to promote scholarly integrity. With other organizations on the UAB campus (like the Center for Clinical and Translational Science), we are collecting and publicizing best practices to strengthen mentoring across the campus. With the CCTS, Dr. Kincaid is developing a centralized website for distributing educational materials for scholarly integrity; the products that we have created will eventually be located on that website. We will continue to engage teaching assistants to develop teaching materials for their undergraduate students in the STEM disciplines; since many of these undergraduate students are working toward further graduate and professional training, these early exposures to "responsible conduct" will prepare them for more advanced education as graduate and professional students. We are also partnering with our sister campuses in the University of Alabama system to develop system wide resources to promote the dialog on scholarly integrity.

Appendix D
Reportable Broad Fields, Subfields, and Disciplines

Reportable Broad Fields	Reportable Subfields	Reportable Disciplines
Education	Education	Education
Humanities and Arts	Foreign Languages and Literatures	Foreign Languages and Literatures
	History	History
Life Sciences	Biological and Biomedical Sciences	Cellular and Molecular Physiology/Cell Biology
		Neuroscience
		Pharmacology and Toxicology
	Health and Medical Sciences/Professions	Nursing
Physical Sciences and Mathematics	Mathematics/Computer and Information Sciences	Statistics
Social Sciences		

Appendix E
Valid Responses for Research Integrity Inventory Survey by Topic and Question

Policy-related Survey Questions

- Is there a departmental committee with responsibility for facilitating the education of all departmental personnel on responsible conduct of research and scholarly activities? n=239

- Does your department/program help to interpret and explain ethical conduct policies and their implementation within your department/program? n=239

- Does your department/program require some component(s) of training (or integrate systematic and continued training) in research and scholarly integrity for graduate students, postdoctoral fellows, faculty, and technical research staff? n=156

- Is communication of responsible research practices to trainees (postdoctoral fellows, graduate students, undergraduate students, technical staff) considered in the tenure and promotion process? n=187

- Does your department or program evaluate/review ethical conduct policies and their implementation? n=154

Practices

- Does your department/program hold forums that address responsible conduct of research and scholarly activities, at least in part?   n=237

- Is information about responsible conduct of research and scholarly practices included on your departmental/program website?   n=239

- Does your department/program promote "difficult discussions" regarding research and scholarly integrity through courses, workshops and/or seminars?   n=236
    An example might be a discussion of what a trainee should do if he/she observes falsification of data in the lab.

- Does your department/program discuss research and scholarly integrity in orientation for new graduate students, new postdoctoral fellows, new faculty, or new technical research staff?   n=182

- Is communication of responsible research practices to trainees (postdoctoral fellows, graduate students, undergraduate students, technical staff) recognized and/or rewarded in other assessments of faculty members?   n=226

Modes of Exposure to Research Integrity and RCR

- How do your faculty learn about the following research and scholarly integrity topics? *(For each of 12 core RCR topics, respondents could select from one of the following: independent research, workshops, printed materials, web-based materials, no resources, or N/A).*

- How do your postdoctoral students learn about the following research and scholarly integrity topics? *(For each of 12 core RCR topics, respondents could select from one of the following: advisor/mentor, workshops, printed materials, web-based materials, no resources, or N/A).*

- How do your graduate students learn about the following research and scholarly integrity topics? *(For each of 12 core RCR topics, respondents could select from one of the following: advisor/mentor, courses, workshops, printed materials, web-based materials, no resources, or N/A).*

The number of usable responses varies by mode of delivery and perspective (range is 148–216)

Appendix F
Resources for
Research Integrity
Program Development
and Enhancement

The PSI website (www.scholarlyintegrity.org) contains an online resource library of materials relevant to those seeking to enhance graduate education in the responsible conduct of research and research and scholarly integrity. These resources have been compiled and arranged primarily with deans and administrators working to implement new, institution-wide structures of education in mind, and secondarily to serve faculty members involved in ethics education and training in the Responsible Conduct of Research and graduate students seeking knowledge on specific topics in research ethics and training.[28] The online library includes resources on general issues and specific topics in research integrity and institutionalization, as well as discipline-specific resources and examples. The online resource library contains a variety of different kinds of resources: sample curricula and course syllabi, case studies, links to video resources, reports, and links to relevant external sources of information about policies and codes of conduct, etc. (http://www.scholarlyintegrity.org/Resources.aspx).[29]

The resources collected below represent a selection from the larger online resource library and are indicative of the depth and breadth of the online resource library. Despite the breadth and number of useful resources accessible through the online PSI resource library, an innovative search engine provides users with an intuitive means of quickly finding relevant resources.

---

28. The America Competes Act resulted in the creation of an NSF-funded national online research ethics library, Ethics Core (http://nationalethicscenter.org/), designed to serve individual RCR program directors, faculty, and students
29. CGS is grateful to AAAS and the National Academies for contributing a significant number of resources on Scientific Misconduct and Research Integrity to the PSI online library

General Resources

Books, Articles, and Reports

Alper, H. (2008, April). How can research integrity be best achieved? *Materials Today*, 11(4), 60. Retrieved from http://www.sciencedirect.com/

American Association for the Advancement of Science (AAAS) and the United States Office of Research Integrity (ORI). (2000). *The role and activities of scientific societies in promoting research integrity: A report on a conference.* Retrieved from http://www.aaas.org/

Anderson, MS (2007). "Collective openness and other recommendations for the promotion of research integrity" *Science and Engineering Ethics* 13(4), 387-394.

Committee on Assessing Integrity in Research Environments, National Research Council, Institute of Medicine. (2002). *Integrity in scientific research: Creating an environment that promotes responsible conduct.* The National Academies Press.

Epstein, D. (2006, April 24). The real science ethics issues. *Inside Higher Ed.* Retrieved from http://www.insidehighered.com/

European Science Foundation. (2007). *Research integrity: Global responsibility to foster common standards.* Science policy briefing. Office of Research Integrity, U.S. Department of Health and Human Services.

Jonas, H. (1984). *The imperative of responsibility: In search of an ethics for the technological age.* Chicago, IL: University of Chicago Press.

Martison, B.C., Anderson, M. S., & de Vries, R. (2005, June 8). Scientists behaving badly. *Nature*, 435, 737-738.

Panel on Scientific Responsibility and the Conduct of Research (1992). *Responsible Science, Volume I: Ensuring the Integrity of the Research Process.* The National Academies Press.

Panel on Scientific Responsibility and the Conduct of Research (1993). *Responsible Science, Volume II: Background Papers and Resource Documents.* The National Academies

Steneck, N. H. (2007). ORI Introduction to the responsible conduct of research. Office of Research Integrity. Retrieved from http://ori.hhs.gov/

Wilkins, A. S. (2008). A matter of standards. I. The individual scientist. *BioEssays,* 30(9), 795-797.

Wilkins, A. S. (2008). A matter of standards. II. Grants and academic positions. *BioEssays,* 30(9), 923-925.

Journals

American Journal of Bioethics. Taylor & Francis and the Center for Practical Bioethics.

Accountability in Research: Policies and Quality Assurance. Taylor & Francis.

Atrium: The Report of the Northwestern Medical Humanities and Bioethics Program. Northwestern University Feinberg School of Medicine.

Hastings Center Report. The Hastings Center.

International Journal of Internet Research Ethics. Center for Information policy Research, School of Information Studies, University of Wisconsin-Milwaukee.

Journal of Empirical Research on Human Research Ethics. University of California Press.

Journal of Law, Medicine, and Ethics. American Society of Law, Medicine and Ethics.

Journal of Research Administration. Society of Research Administrators International.

Kennedy Institute of Ethics Journal. Kennedy Institute of Ethics.

Office of Research Integrity Newsletter. Office of Research Integrity.

Research Ethics. Sage Journals.

Science and Engineering Ethics. Springer.

Science Magazine. American Association for the Advancement of Science.

Science Progress. Center for American Progress.

Visual and Web Resources

American Association for the Advancement of Science (AAAS) (1996; updated in 2000). *Integrity in Scientific Research.* Videos. Retrieved from http://www.aaas.org/spp/video/

Atlanta Clinical and Translational Science Institute Ethics Center. Website. Retrieved from http://www.actsi.org/

Ethics and Research in the Community. Bryn Mawr College and the Massachusetts College of Pharmacy and Health Sciences. Website. Retrieved from http://www.brynmawr.edu/grants/RCR/

Ethics Day: Engaging librarians in the responsible conduct of research. (2010, October). Conference Proceedings, University of Massachusetts, Amherst. Retrieved from http://guides.library.umass.edu/

Globethics.net. Website. Retrieved from http://www.globethics.net/

Global Ethics Observatory (GEObs). UNESCO. Website. Retrieved from http://www.unesco.org/

Integrity in Science Database. Center for Science in the Public Interest. Website. Retrieved from http://www.cspinet.org/integrity/

Office of Research Integrity. United States Department of Health and Human Services. Website. Retrieved from http://ori.hhs.gov/

Resources of Research Ethics Education. University of California, San Diego. Website. Retrieved from http://research-ethics.net/index/

University of Kansas. Research Integrity. Website. Retrieved from http://www2.ku.edu/~rcr/

Plagiarism

Anderson, M. S. and Steneck, N. H.(2011, January). The problem of plagiarism. *Official journal of the society of urologic oncology,* 29 (1), 90-94.

Bilic-Zulle, L., Azman, J., Frkovic, V. & Petrovecki, M. (2008). Is there an effective approach to deterring students from plagiarizing? *Science and Engineering Ethics,* 14(1), 1353-3452.

Bouville, M. (2008). Plagiarism: Words and ideas. *Science and Engineering Ethics,* 14(3), 311-322. Retrieved from http://www.springerlink.com/

Cicutto, L. (2008). Plagiarism: Avoiding the peril in scientific writing. *Chest,* 133(2), 579-81. Retrieved from http://www.chestjournal.org/

Couzin-Frankel, J. and Grom, J. (2009, May 22). Scientific publishing: Plagiarism sleuths. *Science,* 23, 325(5930), 1004-1007.

Office of Research Integrity (ORI). (1994). ORI Policy on plagiarism. Retrieved from http://ori.hhs.gov/

Office of Research Integrity (ORI). (2011). Publications/Authorship. Retrieved from http://ori.hhs.gov/

Plagiary: Cross-disciplinary studies in plagiarism, fabrication, and falsification. University of Michigan Library. Retrieved from http://quod.lib. umich.edu/p/plag/

Triggle, C. R. and Triggle, D. J. What is the future of peer review? Why is there fraud in science? Is plagiarism out of control? Why do scientists do bad things? Is it all a case of: "All that is necessary for the triumph of evil is that good men do nothing?" (2007, February). *Vascular Health Risk Management,* 3(1), 39-53.

Data Management

Committee on Responsibilities of Authorship in the Biological Sciences, National Research Council (2003). *Sharing Publication-Related Data and Materials: Responsibilities of Authorship in the Life Sciences.* The National Academies Press.

Fanelli, D. (2009, May). How many scientists fabricate and falsify research? A systematic review and meta-analysis of survey data. *Plos One,* 4(5), e5738. doi:10.1371/journal.pone.0005738

National Institutes of Health. (2003). Data sharing policy. Retrieved from http://grants.nih.gov/

National Institute of Medicine. (2000). Protecting data privacy in health services research. Washington, D. C.: National Academies Press.

Office of Research Integrity (ORI). (2012). Data management. Retrieved from http://ori.hhs.gov/

Special Issue: Responsible Data Management. (2010). *Science and Engineering Ethics,* 16 (4).

Taylor, H. A., Chaisson, L., & Sugarman, J. (2008). Enhancing communication among data monitoring committees and institutional review boards. *Clinical Trials* 5(3), 277-82.

Welsh, R. K., Lareau, C. R., Clevenger, J. K., & Reger, M. A. (2008). Ethical and legal considerations regarding disputed authorship with the use of shared data. *Accountability in Research: Policies & Quality Assurance,* 15(2), 105-131.

Van den Broeck, J., Argeseanu Cunningham, S., Eeckels, R., & Herbst, K. (2005). Data cleaning: Detecting, diagnosing, and editing data abnormalities. *PLoS Medicine, 2*(10), e267. doi:10.1371/journal.pmed.0020267

Conflicts of Interest

Ancker, J.S., and Flanagin, A. (2007). "A comparison of conflict of interest policies at peer-reviewed journals in different scientific disciplines." *Science and Engineering Ethics,* 13(2), 147-157.

Duval, G. (2007, February 22-23). Conference on conflicts of interest in research: Summary of proceedings. *Conference on Conflicts of Interest in Research.* The Research Ethics Project.

Elliott, K. C. (2008). Scientific judgment and the limits of conflict-of-interest policies. *Accountability in Research: Policies & Quality Assurance,* 15(1), 1-29. Retrieved from http://www.informaworld.com/

Endocrine Society Ethics Advisory Committee. (2003). Ethical aspects of conflicts of interests. Retrieved from http://www.endo-society.org/

Institute on Medicine as a Profession. (2008). Conflict of interest policy database. Retrieved from http://www.imapny.org/

Malay, D. S. (2008). Conflicts of interest, ghostwriters, and the importance of disclosure. *Journal of Foot and Ankle Surgery,* 47(5), 375-6

Marshall, E. (2008). A bumper crop of conflicts. *Science,* 320(5876), 602.

National Institutes of Health Public-Private Partnerships. (2010). Conflicts of interest policy. Retrieved from http://ppp.od.nih.gov/regulations/

National Science Foundation, Office of Investigations, Office of the Inspector General. (2002, March 15) Conflict of interest considerations. Retrieved from http://www.nsf.gov/oig/coi.pdf

Office of Research Integrity (ORI). (2011). Conflicts of Interest and Commitment. Retrieved from http://ori.hhs.gov/

Whelan, E. (2008, April 8). "Conflict" chills research. *The Washington Times.*

Wirth, S. and Wolfberg, D. (2008). Conflicts of interest: Avoid the appearance of impropriety. *JEMS,* 32(11), 24.

Human Subjects

American Anthropological Association. (2004, June 4). Statement on ethnography and institutional review boards. Retrieved from http://www.aaanet.org

American Educational Research Association. Social and Behavioral Sciences Working Group. Retrieved from http://www.aera.net/

Borenstein, J. (2008). The expanding purview: Institutional review boards and the review of human subjects research. *Accountability in Research: Policies & Quality Assurance,* 15(3), 188-204. Retrieved from http://www.informaworld.com/

Federman, D. D., Hanna, K. E., & Rodriguez, L. L. (Editors.) (2002). *Responsible research: A systems approach to protecting research participants.* Committee on Assessing the System for Protecting Human Research Participants. The National Academies Press.

Frankel, M. S. and Siang, S. (1999). *Ethical and legal aspects of human subjects research on the internet: A report on a workshop.* American Association for the Advancement of Science (AAAS).

Joffe, S. and Miller, F. G. (2008). Bench to bedside: Mapping the moral terrain of clinical research. *The Hastings Center Report,* 38(2), 30-44. Retrieved from http://www.thehastingscenter.org/

Journal of Empirical Research on Human Research Ethics.

Maloney, D. (2010). Major Revisions to Canada's Research Ethics Statement. *Human Research Report,* 25(3), 6. Retrieved from http://www.humanresearchreport.com

National Council on Ethics in Human Research (Canada). Website. Retrieved from http://www.ncehr-cnerh.org/

National Institutes of Health. Human Research Protections Program. Website. Retrieved from http://ohsr.od.nih.gov/

National Research Council. (2003). Protecting participants and facilitating social and behavioral sciences research.

Office of Research Integrity (ORI). (2012). Human subject research. Retrieved from http://ori.hhs.gov/

Public-Private Partnership Program. (2010). Human subjects protection. Retrieved from http://ppp.od.nih.gov/

Health Resources and Services Administration. (2004). Program protection of human subjects participating in research programs conducted or supported by HRSA policy. Retrieved from http://www.hrsa.gov/

Animal Welfare

Palka, J. and Webster, M. (2008, February 29). Animal testing and research ethics. *Science Friday.* National Public Radio.

American Association for Laboratory Animal Science. Website. Retrieved from http://www.aalas.org/

Animal Welfare Act. Title 7 Chapter 54 U.S.C. § 2131—2159 (1966).

Canadian Council on Animal Care in Science. Website. Retrieved from http://www.ccac.ca/en_

Charrow, R. (2010). Law in the laboratory: A guide to the ethics of federally funded science research. Chicago: University of Chicago Press.

Federation of Animal Science Societies. Website. Retrieved from http://www.fass.org/

McNeil, Jr., D. G. (2008, July 11). When human rights extend to nonhumans. *New York Times.*

Office of Laboratory Animal Welfare, National Institutes of Health. Website. Retrieved from http://grants.nih.gov/grants/olaw/olaw.htm

Office of Research Integrity (ORI). (2012). Animal resources. Retrieved from http://ori.hhs.gov/

Olsson, A. S., Hansen, A. K., & Sandøe, P. (2007, September 21). Ethics and refinement in animal research. *Science.* 317(5845). 1680.

Research Misconduct

Boesz, C. and Lloyd, N. (2008). Collaborations: Investigating International Misconduct. *Nature*, 452(7188), 686—687. Retrieved from http://www.nature.com/nature/

Gallup Organization for Office of Research Integrity. (2008, April 8). Final Report: Observing and Reporting Suspected Misconduct in Biomedical Research.

Gawrylewski, A. (March 2009). Fixing fraud: Tips for preventing research misconduct and maintaining the integrity of your research. *The Scientist,* 23(3), 67.

Handelsman, J. (2008). The gray zone: Scientific misconduct comes in many shades. *DNA & Cell Biology,* 27 (2), 63-64.

Heitman, E., Anestidou, L., Olsen, C., & Bulger, R. E. *Hastings Cent Rep*, 35(5), 49.

Lind, R. A., Lepper, T. S. (2007). Sensitivity to research misconduct: A conceptual model. *Medical Law,* 26(3), 585-98.

National Science Foundation. Research misconduct regulation. Key Regulations. Retrieved from http://www.nsf.gov/

Office of Research Integrity (ORI). (2011). Definition of research misconduct. Retrieved from http://ori.hhs.gov/

Office of Science and Technology Policy (OSTP). (2000, December 6). Federal research misconduct policy. Federal Register. 65(235), 76260-76264.

Pryor, E. R., Habermann, B. & Broome, M. E. (2007). Scientific misconduct from the perspective of research coordinators: A national survey." *Journal of Medical Ethics,* 33(6), 365-369.

Steneck, N. H. (2006). Fostering integrity in research: Definitions, current knowledge, and future directions. *Science and Engineering Ethics*, 12(1), 53-74.

UK Research Integrity Office. Website. Retrieved from http://www.ukrio.org/

Workshop Participants. (2007, July 19). Unofficial report on workshop on best practices for ensuring scientific integrity and preventing misconduct, 4th Draft. *World Conference on Research Integrity*.

Publication/Authorship

American Chemical Society. (2012, June). Ethical guidelines to publication of chemical research. Retrieved from http://pubs.acs.org/

Funk, C. L., Barrett, K. A., & Macrina, F. L. (2007). Authorship and publication practices: Evaluation of the effect of responsible conduct of research instruction to postdoctoral trainees. *Accountability in Research*, 14 (4), 269–305.

Louis K. S., Holdsworth, J. M., Anderson, M. S., Campbell, E. G. (2008). Everyday ethics in research: Translating authorship guidelines into practice in the bench sciences. *Journal of Higher Education,* 79 (1), 88-112.

Plemmons, D. (2011, April 27). A broader discussion of authorship. *Science and Engineering Ethics,* 27.

Siedlecki, S. L., Montague, M., & Schultz, J. (2008). Writing for publication: Avoiding common ethical pitfalls. *Journal of Wound, Ostomy & Continence Nursing,* 35(2), 147-150.

Wager, E. (2007). Ethical publishing: The innocent author's guide to avoiding misconduct. *Menopause International,* 13(3), 98-102.

Mentorship

AAMC Group on Graduate Research, Education, and Training (GREAT). (2006, December). Compact between postdoctoral appointees and their mentors. Association of American Medical Colleges (AAMC).

Bird, S. J. and Sprague, R. L. (2001). Mentoring and responsible conduct of research: Reflections and future. *Science and Engineering Ethics,* 7(4), 451-3.

Daroff, R. B. (2007). Report from the Scientific Integrity Advisor: Issues arising in 2005 and 2006. *Neurology,* 68(21), 1841-2.

Hughes, C., Boyd, E., & Dykstra, S. J. (2010, November). Evaluation of a university-based mentoring program: Mentors' perspectives on a service-learning experience. *Mentoring & Tutoring: Partnership in Learning,* 18(4), 361-382.

Lapidus, J. and Mishkin, B. (1994). Values and ethics in the graduate education of scientists. *American Journal of Pharmaceutical Education,* 58(1994), 333-338.

McGee, R., Almquist, J., Keller, J. L., & Jacobsen, S. J. (2008). Teaching and learning responsible research conduct: Influences of prior experiences on acceptance of new ideas. *Accountability in Research: Policies & Quality Assurance,* 15(1), 30-62.

Mitchell, T and J Carroll (2008). "Academic and research misconduct in the PhD: issues for students and supervisors." *Nurse Education Today,* 28(2), 218-26.

National Academy of Sciences, National Academy of Engineering, and Institute of Medicine. (1997). Adviser, teacher, role model, friend: On being a mentor to students in science and engineering. Washington, D.C.: National Academy Press.

National Institutes of Health. (1999). A Guide to Training and Mentoring in the Intramural Research Program at NIH. Retrieved from http://sourcebook.od.nih.gov/ethic-conduct/mentor-guide.htm

Office of Research Integrity (ORI). (2012). Mentorship. Retrieved from http://ori.hhs.gov/

Wright, S. L. T. and Cornelison, J. B. (2008, September). *Science and Engineering Ethics,* 14 (3), 323-36

Peer Review

Alberts, B., Hanson, B., & Kelner, K. L. (2008). Reviewing Peer Review. *Science* 321(5885), 15. Retrieved from http://www.sciencemag.org/

DeAngelis, C. D. and Thornton, J. P. (2008). Preserving confidentiality in the peer review process. *JAMA,* 299(16), 1956.

DuBois, J. M. (2009). The Biomedical Ethics Ontology Proposal: Excellent aims, questionable methods. *Journal of Empirical Research on Human Research Ethics*, 4(1), 59-62.

Minion, D., Sorial, E., & Endean, E. (2007). Ethics of guidelines for reviewers of medical manuscripts. *Journal of Vascular Surgery,* 46(2), 391-3.

Nature's peer review debate. *Nature.* Retrieved from http://www.nature.com/

Office of Research Integrity (ORI). (2011). Peer review. Retrieved from http://ori.hhs.gov/

Resnik, D. B., Guiterrez-Ford, C., & Peddada, S. (2008). Perceptions of ethical problems with scientific journal peer review: An exploratory study. *Science and Engineering Ethics,* 14(3), 305-310.

Rodriguez, M. A., Bollen, J., & Van de Sompel, H. (2006). The convergence of digital libraries and the peer-reviewed process. *Journal of Information Science*, 32(2), 149-159.

Collaboration

Anderson, M. S. and Steneck, N. H. (Eds.) (2010). *International research collaborations: Much to be gained, many ways to get in trouble.* New York and London: Routledge.

Aulisio, M.P. and Arnold, R. M. (2008). "Role of the ethics committee: helping to address value conflicts or uncertainties." *Chest*, 134(2), 417-24. Retrieved from http://www.ncbi.nlm.nih.gov/

Boesz, C. and Lloyd, N. (2008). Collaborations: Investigating International Misconduct. *Nature*, 452(7188), 686—687.

Broome, M. E. (2007). Collaboration: The devil's in the detail. *Nursing Outlook*, 55(1), 1-2.

Callister, L. C., Getmanenko, N.I., Khalaf, I., Garvrish, N., Semenic, S., Vehvilainen-Jukunen, K., and Turkina, N. V. (2008, January-February). Collaborative International Research. *Journal of Continuing Education in Nursing*, 37: 1.

Chaplin C. (2006). Ethics of international clinical research collaboration--the experience of AlloStem. *International Journal of Immunogenetics*, 33 (1), 1-5.

Government-University-Industry Research Roundtable. (1999). Overcoming barriers to collaborative research: Report of a workshop. Washington, D.C.: National Academy Press.

Ledford, H. (2008, April 10). Collaborations: With all good intentions. *Nature* 452, 682-684.

Loo K.K. (2009). Procedural challenges in international collaborative research. *Academic psychiatry: the journal of the American Association of Directors of Psychiatric Residency Training and the Association for Academic Psychiatry*, 33(3), 229-33.

Office of Research Integrity (ORI). (2012). Collaborative science. Retrieved from http://ori.hhs.gov/

Philpott, J. (2010, March). Applying themes from research ethics to international educational partnerships. *Virtual Mentor*, 12(3), 171-178. Retrieved from http://virtualmentor.ama-assn.org/

Sadrozinski, R. (2005). *Evaluative framework for international collaboration: Final report to the National Science Foundation* Center for Innovation in Research and Graduate Education. (CIRGE). Retrieved from http://depts.washington.edu/cirgeweb

.

Sloan, S. S. & Arrison, T. (2011). *Examining core elements of international research collaboration.* Washington, DC: National Academies Press.

Financial and Personnel Management

Doucet, M., and Sismondo, S. (2008). Evaluating solutions to sponsorship bias. *Journal of Medical Ethics* 34(8), 627-30. Retrieved from https://www.researchgate.net/

Kvaal, S. I. (2008). Ethical and legal considerations in a case of research fraud. *Journal of the American College of Dentists,* 75(2), 29-35.

Martinson, B. C., Crain, A. L., Anderson, M. S., & De Vries, R. (2009, November). Institutions' expectations for researchers' self-funding, federal grant holding, and private industry involvement: Manifold drivers of self-interest and researcher behavior. *Academic Medicine,* 84(11), 1491–1499.

Mastroianni, A. C., Faden, R., and Federman, D. (Editors). Committee on the Ethical and Legal Issues Relating to the Inclusion of Women in Clinical Studies, Institute of Medicine. (1999). *Women and health research: Ethical and legal issues of including women in clinical studies.* Volume 2, Workshop and Commissioned Papers. The National Academies Press

Washington State University. Administration and Fiscal Management. Website. Retrieved from http://www.ogrd.wsu.edu/ori/fiscal.html

Ethical Deliberation and Training

Alexander, M. and Williams, W. R. (2004). *A guidebook for teaching selected responsible conduct of research topics to a culturally diverse trainee group.* Washington, DC: Office of Research Integrity.

Deming, N., Fryer-Edwards, K., Dudzinski, D., Starks, H., Culver, J., Hopley, E., Robins, L., & Burke, W. (2007). Incorporating principles and practical wisdom in research ethics education: A preliminary study. *Academic Medicine,* 82 (1), 18-23.

Kalichman, M. W. (2007). Responding to challenges in educating for the responsible conduct of research. *Academic Medicine*, 82(9), 870-5.

Macrina, F. L. (2007). Scientific societies and promotion of the responsible conduct of research: codes, policies, and education. *Academic Medicine,* 82(9), 865-9.

Olson L.E. (2010). Developing a Framework for Assessing Responsible Conduct of Research Education Programs. *Science and Engineering Ethics*, 16 (1), 185-200.

Resources of Research Ethics Education. University of California, San Diego. Retrieved from http://research-ethics.net/index/

Steneck, N. H., Bulger, R. E. (2007, September). The history, purpose, and future of instruction in the responsible conduct of research. *Academic Medicine*, 82 (9), 829-834.

Whistleblowing

American Association for the Advancement of Science and the Office of Research Integrity. (2000). Responding to allegations of research misconduct: Inquiry, investigation, and outcomes: A practicum. Washington, D.C.: AAAS and ORI.

Goldenring, J. R. (2010). Perspective: Innocence and due diligence: Managing unfounded allegations of scientific misconduct. *Academic Medicine,* 85(3), 527-530.

Gunsalus C. K. (1998). How to blow the whistle and still have a career afterwards. *Science and Engineering Ethics,* 4(5), 1-64.

Keith-Spiegel, P., Sieber, J., & Koocher, G.P. (2010). *Responding to research wrong-doing: A user-friendly guide.* Office of Research Integrity (ORI).

Lind R. A. and Lepper, T. S. (2007). Sensitivity to research misconduct: A conceptual model. *Medical Law,* 26(3), 585-98.

Long, T. C., Errami, M., George, A. C., Sun, Z., Garner, H. R. (2009, March 6). Responding to possible plagiarism. *Science, 323,* 1293-94.

Image Manipulation

Hendricks, M. (2011, January). Scientific integrity in the age of Photoshop. Johns Hopkins Institute for Basic Biomedical Science. Retrieved from http://www.hopkinsmedicine.org/

Kremenak, N. (2008). Images: To alter or not to alter? The ethics of image modification. *Journal of Prosthodontics,* 17(1), 79-80.

Parish, D. and Noonan, B. (2009, January 6) Image Manipulation as Research Misconduct. *Science and Engineering Ethics.* Retrieved from http://www.springerlink.com/

Approaches to Institutional Change

Barnes, B. E., Friedman, Charles, P., Rosenberg, J. L., Russell, J., Beedle, A., & Levine, A. S. (2006, February). Creating an infrastructure for training in the responsible conduct of research: The University of Pittsburgh's experience. *Academic Medicine,* 81(2), 119-127.

Bulger, R.E. and Heitman, E. (2007). Expanding responsible conduct of research instruction across the university. *Academic Medicine,* 82(9), 876-8.

Carlin, D. and Denecke, D. (2008). *Best practices in graduate education for the responsible conduct of research.* Washington, DC: Council of Graduate Schools.

Committee on Assessing Integrity in Research Environments. (2002, July). *Integrity in scientific research: Creating an environment that promotes responsible conduct.* Washington, DC: National Research Council, Institute of Medicine.

Denecke, D. (2008, June). The Compelling Need for a Comprehensive Approach to Scholarly Integrity. *Communicator,* 41(5). Council of Graduate Schools.

DuBois, J. M. (2004). Is compliance a professional virtue of researchers? Reflections on promoting the responsible conduct of research. *Ethics and Behavior,* 14(4), 383-395.

Gallant, T. B. (2011). *Creating the ethical academy: A systems approach to understanding misconduct and empowering change.* New York: Routledge.

Gunsalus, C. K. (1998). Preventing the need for whistleblowing: Practical advice for university administrators. *Science and Engineering Ethics,* 4, 75-94.

Martinson, B. C., Crain, A. L., Anderson, M. S., & De Vries, R. (2009). Institutions' expectations for researchers' self-funding, federal grant holding, and private industry involvement: Manifold drivers of self-interest and researcher behavior. *Academic Medicine,* 84(11), 1491–1499.

Martinson, B. C., Crain, A. L., De Vries, R., & Anderson, M. S. (2010, September). The importance of organizational justice in ensuring research integrity. *Journal of Empirical Research on Human Research Ethics: An International Journal,* 5(3), 67-83.

Office of Research Integrity. (2005). *Requirements for institutional policies and procedures on research misconduct under the new PHS Policies on Research Misconduct.* Washington, D.C.: U.S. Department of Health and Human Services.

Palmer, P. J. (2007, November/December). A new professional: The aims of education revisited. *Change Magazine.*

Public Responsibility in Medicine and Research. (2010, April 8). *Educating for the Responsible Conduct of Research (RCR): Strategies for Research Institutions.* Webinar. Retrieved from http://www.primr.org/

Vasgird, D. R. (2007). Prevention over Cure: the Administrative Rationale for Education in the Responsible Conduct of Research. *Academic Medicine,* 82(9), 835-83.

Wilson, K., Schreier, A., Griffin, A., & Resnik, D. (2007). Research records and the resolution of misconduct allegations at research universities. *Accountability in Research,* 14(1), 57-71.

Program Assessment

Denecke, D. and Kent, J. (2011, June). An update on the Project for Scholarly Integrity and new tools in the RCR toolbox. *Communicator,* 44 (5), 6-8. Council of Graduate Schools.

DuBois, J. M., Dueker, J. M., Anderson, E. E., Campbell, J. (2008). Development and assessment of a NIH-funded research ethics training program. *Academic Medicine*, 83(6): 596-603. 2008.

Kalichman, M. W. and Plemmons, D. K. Reported goals for responsible conduct of research courses. *Academic Medicine*, 82(9), 846-852.

Kon, A. A., Schilling, D. A., Heitman, E., Steneck, N. H., & DuBois, J. M. (2011, January). Content analysis of major textbooks and online resources used in responsible conduct of research instruction. *AJOB Primary Research*, 2(1), 42-46.

Olsen, L. E. (2010). Developing a framework for assessing responsible conduct of research education programs. *Science and Engineering Ethics* 16(1): 185-200. 2010.

Powell, S. T., Allison, M. A., & Kalichman, M. W. (2007). Effectiveness of a responsible conduct of research course: a preliminary study. *Science and Engineering Ethics*, 13.2, 249-264.

Learning Assessment

Antes, A. L., Murphy, S. T., Waples, E. P., Mumford, M. D., Brown, R. P., Connelly, S., & Devenport, L. D. (2009). A meta-analysis of ethics instruction effectiveness in the sciences. *Ethics & Behavior*, 19(5). 379-402.

Debruin, D., Scholder, S. L., Kahn, J., Mastroianni, A. C., Marshall, M. F., Lantos, J. & Sugarman, J. (2007). Educational approaches to the responsible conduct of clinical research: An exploratory study. *Academic Medicine,* 82(1), 32-39.

DuBois, J. M., and Dueker, J. M. (2009). Teaching and assessing the responsible conduct of research: A Delphi consensus panel report. *Journal of Research Administration*, XL(1): 49-70.

Heitman, E., Bulger, R. E. (2006). Assessing educational literature in responsible conduct of research for core content. *Accountability in Research*, 12, 207-224.

Kligyte, V., Marcy, R. T., Sevier, S. T., Godfrey, E. S., & Mumford, M. D. (2008). A qualitative approach to responsible conduct of research (RCR) training development: Identification of metacognitive strategies. *Science and Engineering Ethics,* 14 (1), 3-31.

Pimple, K. D. (2001, October). *Assessing teaching and learning in the responsible conduct of research.* Background paper. Washington, D.C.: Institute of Medicine Committee on Assessing Integrity in Research Environments.

Pimple, K. D. (2001, April). *Assessing student learning in the responsible conduct of research.* Bloomington, IN: Poynter Center for the Study of Ethics and American Institutions, Indiana University.

Wessell, C. B. Evaluation of a self-paced learning module to teach responsible literature searching for research. *Journal of the Medical Library Association* 98(1), 82-85.

Climate Assessment

Anderson, M. S. (2010). Research misconduct and misbehavior in relation to the research environment. Found in *Creating the ethical academy: A systems approach to understanding misconduct and empowering change.* New York: Routledge.

Louis, K.S., Holdsworth, J. M., Anderson, M. S., & Campbell, E. G. (2007). Becoming a scientist: The effects of work-group size and organizational climate. *Journal of Higher Education,* 78 (3), 311-336.

Mumford, M. D., Waples, E. P., Antes, A. L., Murphy, S. T., Connelly, S., Brown, R. P., & Devenport, L.D. (2009). Exposure to unethical career events: Effects on decision making, climate, and socialization. *Ethics & Behavior,* 19(5), 351-378.

Pickett, M., (2007). Theory of reasoned action: Reassessing the relationships of moral and ethical climates in organizations. *Journal of American Society of Business and Behavioral Science,* 3(1), 90-99.

Thrush, C. R., Vander Putten, J., Rapp, C. G., Pearson, L. C., Berry, K. S., & O'Sullivan, P. S. (2007, December). Content validation of the organizational climate for research integrity. *Journal of Empirical Research on Human Research Ethics,* 2(4), 35-52.

Thrush, C. R., Martinson, B.C., Crain, A.L., & Wells, J.A. (2011, March). *User's manual for the survey of organizational research climate.* Retrieved from https://sites.google.com/site/surveyoforgresearchclimate/

Thrush, C. R., Putten, J. V., Rapp, C. G., Pearson, L. C., Berry, K. S., & O'Sullivan, P. S. (2007). Content validation of the organizational climate for research integrity (OCRI) survey. *Journal of Empirical Research on Human Research Ethics, 2*(4), 35-52. doi:10.1525/jer.2007.2.4.35

Webber, S. (2007, September). Ethical climate typology and question-naire: A discussion of instrument modifications. *The Journal of Academic Librarianship, 33*(5), 567-580.

Related Publications from the Council of Graduate Schools

Best Practices in Graduate Education for the Responsible Conduct of Research (2009)

This publication documents the results of a collaborative project, supported by a grant from NSF, between CGS and eight universities to identify best practices in the development of research ethics programs for graduate students in science and engineering. Topics addressed include curricular approaches, program sustainability, considerations specific to master's-focused institutions, and assessment.

ITEM NUMBER: BPRCR
MEMBER PRICE: $15 | NON-MEMBER PRICE: $18
*Bulk pricing available to members only

Graduate Education for the Responsible Conduct of Research (2006)

This CGS publication identifies "best practices" in responsible conduct of research (RCR) education and is aimed at helping graduate deans, department chairs, and faculty members establish and sustain educational programs that foster RCR on their campuses.

ITEM NUMBER: GRADRCR
MEMBER PRICE: $15 | NON-MEMBER PRICE: $18
*Bulk pricing available to members only

To order publications, please visit www.cgsnet.org and click on 'Publications.'